The Way of Jesus

Many today are curious about the life of Jesus. What
is the truth about the stories of his life, his teaching,
his death – and rising again? How can we understand
them today?

This book is written for the many who simply want
to find out about the life and teaching of Jesus,
founder of Christianity. The author has lived for
many years in the Middle East, and has experienced
at first hand both the misunderstandings about Jesus
and people's curiosity about who he really was.

Dr Bruce Farnham is a scientist by training. He has
written for others who, like himself, are living and
working in a world which is both increasingly secular
and also torn by religious ideologies. It is vital that
people from many backgrounds, especially those
from other religions, understand the facts and
fallacies about the life of Jesus, and how his message
is understood today.

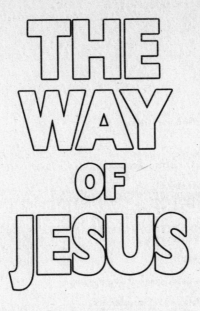

THE WAY OF JESUS

DR BRUCE FARNHAM

A LION PAPERBACK
Tring • Batavia • Sydney

Copyright © 1986 Bruce Farnham

Published by
Lion Publishing plc
Icknield Way, Tring, Herts, England
ISBN 0 7459 1452 7
Albatross Books Pty Ltd
PO Box 320, Sutherland, NSW 2232, Australia
ISBN 0 86760 961 3

First published 1986
This edition published 1988

British Library Cataloguing in Publication Data
Farnham, Bruce
   The way of Jesus. — (A Lion paperback).
   1. Jesus Christ — Biographies
   I. Title
   232.9′01
   ISBN 0 7459 1452 7

Library of Congress Cataloging-in-Publication Data
Farnham, Bruce.
   The way of Jesus/Bruce Farnham.
      p. cm. — (A Lion paperback)
   ISBN 0 7459 1452 7 (pbk.)
   1. Jesus Christ — Biography.
   2. Christian biography — Palestine.
I. Title.
BT301.2.F375   1988
232.9′01 — dc19
[B]

Printed and bound in Great Britain by
Cox & Wyman Ltd, Reading

Contents

Introduction

People coming to so-called Christian countries are often surprised to find how little the people know about the founder of the Christian faith.

The reason is simple. Many people have the word 'Christian' written on their identity card or birth certificate. But they are Christian only in name, not in reality. Even if they believe in God, few know much about Jesus, the founder of Christianity.

I have written this book because of the difficulty of obtaining basic information on the life and teachings of Jesus. Most people do not have the time or energy to read long theological books. But everyone should have some knowledge of the great religious leaders of the world.

Let me say immediately that I am a scientist and not a theologian. For this reason I have tried to write a book which is relevant to people like myself who are living and working in the secular world.

I must also say that although I am a scientist by training, I am not an unbiased observer when it comes to the life and teachings of Jesus. My own life has been deeply changed by both his life and his teachings. But I think you would prefer to read about Jesus from a friend rather than an enemy. Enemies do not make good biographers.

Although I am certainly not unbiased, I have tried to write as objectively as possible. Many of my friends are from different religious backgrounds to my own. Some do not believe in God at all. So I have tried to give an account which is relevant to people of widely different backgrounds. If I offend anyone in the process, then I am sorry, but I am sure you would prefer me to present what Jesus himself taught, even though his claims may seem shocking to some.

I have tried to present in this book what the great majority of

Christians throughout the world believe about Jesus Christ. Every religion has very extreme sects which do not represent the generally-accepted beliefs in that religion, and Christianity is no exception. But what I want to present here are Christian beliefs taught by all the main churches down the centuries.

The source of these beliefs is to be found in the New Testament, called the Injil by Muslims, and if you are really serious about studying the life of Jesus then clearly it is essential to read the New Testament. In many places I have put references to the New Testament so that you can look them up if you are interested. The New Testament is the second part of the Bible and was written down over the period AD 45–95. It consists of eye-witness accounts of the life and teachings of Jesus written by those who knew him, together with various letters written to the early churches. When giving a reference to the New Testament, the name of the book is given first followed by the chapter and then the verse. These chapters and verse numbers were not in the original New Testament but were added later to help in finding specific passages.

I have also included some illustrations which are clearly imaginary. People with whom I live in the Middle East enjoy a story told to illustrate a point. I apologize to others for whom these may be a distraction! You will notice that I generally refer to Jesus without giving him any special title before or after his name. This is not out of disrespect. It is simply that I believe *real* respect is shown to Jesus, not by giving him special titles, but by considering seriously what he taught.

The teachings of Jesus have now spread out from the Middle East to many different countries of the world. Many people have misunderstood parts of the life and teachings of Jesus simply because they have never experienced the Middle East for themselves. I would like to express my indebtedness to my many Arab friends for helping me to look at Jesus in his own historical and cultural context.

1

The Birth and Early Life of Jesus

Jesus Christ was born in about 4 BC in a small town called Bethlehem in Palestine. Although BC stands for 'Before Christ', the exact date of his birth is not known. This is because of some mistakes made as early as the sixth century in calculating the years which had passed since Jesus' birth. However, it is known that Jesus was born in the reign of King Herod[1] and that Herod died in 4 BC. It is likely that Jesus was born shortly before Herod died.

At the time Jesus was born, Palestine was under Roman rule. It was a small state on the eastern boundary of the Roman Empire. Though small it had strategic importance from a military point of view because it was on the edge of the empire and so formed a buffer-state against Rome's enemies. For this reason the state was heavily occupied by Roman soldiers and any opposition to Rome was ruthlessly crushed.

The people living then in Palestine reacted to imperialism in the same kinds of ways as people do today. Some were involved in direct action against the Romans. For example, there was a guerrilla movement called the 'Zealots' which tried to fight Roman rule by armed attacks on military personnel. Simon, one of the followers of Jesus, was called 'the Zealot' and may have come from this group. Other people became involved in parties which were more pacifist but strongly nationalistic. They stressed the importance of observing Jewish religious practices, realizing that this would preserve the Jews' identity as a nation. One of the largest of these groups was called the Pharisees. The Pharisees took the laws of Moses and tried to make them apply to every tiny detail of everyday life. A rival group called the Sadducees were equally religious but were mainly from the upper classes and extremely conservative. They were very scared of political protest because they thought this would only get them into trouble with the Roman authorities.

The great majority of people in Palestine were not involved in any of these groups. They simply wanted to live a quiet life, hoping that one day the colonial power of Rome would collapse and their freedom would be restored. Many believed that a great political deliverer was going to come and save them from the might of Rome. But generally they kept these hopes to themselves. Talking was dangerous and the secret police were strong.

The birth of Jesus

The parents of Jesus came from Nazareth, a small hillside town about 110 kilometres/68 miles north of Bethlehem. His father's name was Joseph and his mother's name was Mary. Jesus was born in Bethlehem and not Nazareth because a census required all adults to register in the towns where their ancestors had lived. The Romans, like most military powers, placed a great emphasis on efficiency and organization. So the Emperor Caesar Augustus gave orders that a census should be taken of the entire Roman world.[2] The census probably took many years to complete. In several places it was resisted because of the disruption it brought to daily life and because of the greater power over the people that its findings would give to the Roman authorities. Each family had to return to the father's original home to make the counting more efficient. Since Joseph came from a family which was descended from King David, he and Mary were forced to travel to Bethlehem, the town from which David originally came.[3]

At the time of the census Joseph was engaged to Mary, but not yet married. Some time before this he had been startled to find that Mary was pregnant. At first, he had wanted to break the engagement because of the shame and rejection that would come from their community once this became public knowledge.[4] But an angel came to Joseph and assured him that the conception was a direct work of God's Spirit.[5] The same angel also told Joseph that he was to call the coming baby Jesus, 'because he will save his people from their sins'.[6] The word 'Jesus' is the Greek form of the Hebrew 'Jeshua' which means 'the Lord saves'. So from the beginning it was clear that Jesus was going to be someone remarkable, not only because of the special manner of his conception, but also because he was to be a 'saviour'. But what kind of saviour was he to be? A dynamic new leader who would overthrow the might of imperial Rome? Or a prophet who would bring the people back to a purer worship of God?

Christians sometimes talk about the 'virgin birth' of Jesus. But his birth was very normal. It was the conception that was so remarkable. Can we accept such a miraculous conception in the light of modern science?

The answer to that question depends on what you believe about God. If you believe in a God who is a Creator, one who is constantly making and keeping going by his power the whole physical world, then it is not too difficult to believe that he can work occasionally in a different way than the way he normally works. This 'unusual' work of God we call a 'miracle'. Our bodies already contain hundreds of millions of cells, but this abnormal event would involve God making one extra cell outside the normal process of meiotic cell division. Because this is unusual we call it a 'miracle', but this does not mean that it is any less or more the work of God than his activity in the rest of our cells.

Science can cope only with what is observable and reproducible. The scientific method is possible only because God has made a logical world in which we observe consistent laws. So, if God chooses to do something highly unusual, it is not a question of 'faith contradicting science' — simply that science is inadequate to examine a rare historical event. It is not science that we should be thinking about when considering a miracle, but the question whether the eyewitness of the event is trustworthy in what he reports.

If we start with the virgin conception and end up discussing biology, then we have missed the point. For here at this moment in time God is giving us a vital clue. His powerful Holy Spirit so worked in Mary's body that fertilization of an ovum occurred quite outside all normal processes. From the beginning of the human race until that point in time there had been genetic continuity. Now suddenly there breaks in a discontinuity. Something totally new is happening which has never happened before. From

that tiny insignificant speck a dynamic power is about to break
out, a power far greater than the mere splitting of an atom.
Something has begun to happen which is both deeply human and
intensely divine.

All Mary knew as she bounced along on the donkey from
Nazareth to Bethlehem was that she was nine months pregnant
and hoping that she would not be forced to deliver the baby by
the roadside. But deep in her heart she had the assurance of God
that everything would be all right. For an angel had appeared to
her too, a few months previously, and told her that she had found
favour with God. She also had been told that the baby would be
called Jesus. But the angel had said some other extraordinary
things to her which would for ever be etched upon her mind.[7] As
she and Joseph travelled along the dusty tracks, a deep, warm
glow of excitement would have touched Mary's face. She must
have felt something inside her even more profound than the stir-
rings of a baby about to be born.

When she and Joseph finally arrived in Bethlehem the town
was already crowded with people returning for the census. But
the picture of Joseph and Mary going from hotel to hotel, and of
being turned away by angry hotel managers until they were
forced to stay in an animal shed outside, is probably a product of
tradition, not an accurate representation. Most of the pictures on
Christmas cards have little to do either with the historical
evidence concerning the birth of Jesus or with peasant life in first-
century Palestine. The tradition is based on the words in Luke 2:7
which are translated 'because there was no room for Mary and
Joseph in the inn'. But the word used there for 'inn' could equally
be translated 'guest-room', and indeed the same word is translated 'guest-room' later on in Luke's Gospel.[8]

So it seems very likely that Joseph and Mary did what anyone
would do in a community practising that hospitality for which
the Middle East is rightly famous. On arriving in Bethlehem they
went immediately to stay with Joseph's relatives. The house
would have been a typical one-roomed home with a guest-room
attached. Both the family and the animals were housed in the
lower part of the main room at night. During the daytime the

animals were of course let out to pasture. A gently-sloping floor led from the higher part of the room, which is where the family slept, to the lower side of the house where the animals were kept at night. On this side there was a raised area, and set into this stone ledge was the 'manger', the basin-shaped opening which was filled with straw for the animals.

It seems that Joseph's relatives already had guests staying with them and the guest-room was occupied. So, Joseph and Mary were welcomed right into the heart of the Palestinian home and stayed in the living-room of the house. We read that when Jesus was born, he was placed in a manger[9] which, full of clean, dry straw, was the ideal place for a new-born baby and quite probably a normal place to put babies when the animals were out-side in pasture.

So far from Joseph and Mary being shunned and left out in the cold, we have a picture of them which is exactly the opposite; they were drawn into the centre of the family. And it was there at the centre of the family in a typical peasant home of first-century Palestine that Jesus was born.

Jesus' early years

Whenever there is a birth, especially of the first-born (and a son at that!), there must be visitors. It was not long before the first visitors began to arrive at the home of Joseph's relatives to bring their congratulations. But what visitors! The birth of Jesus passed entirely unnoticed by the religious and political authori-ties, at least at the beginning. There was no particular reason anyway why they should take any notice of a mere carpenter's new-born baby. Rather it was to a group of shepherds that an angel came to deliver the news of Jesus' birth.[10] The shepherds were terrified by the sudden brightness of the angel's appearance but soon hurried off to the nearby town of Bethlehem to pay their respects at the home of Joseph's relatives.

So begins a pattern which we notice throughout the life of Jesus. God revealed himself not to the top religious or political leaders, not to those who thought they knew all the answers, but rather to the poor and humble.

Once the shepherds had visited Jesus, they quickly spread the word around Bethlehem concerning what they had heard and seen.[11] The shepherds reported that the angel had told them this tiny new-born baby was not only a saviour, but was actually the long-awaited Messiah! The word 'Messiah' is a Hebrew word meaning 'the anointed one'. The Greek word 'Christ' has the same meaning. The coming of the Messiah had been promised centuries before in ancient Jewish writings known as the Tawrat and Zabur, parts of what Christians call the Old Testament. Some people believed that the Messiah was going to come as a great political leader who would deliver Palestine from Roman imperialism. So it was hardly surprising that the people were amazed at the shepherds' report. Were these ignorant shepherds really trying to tell them that this tiny baby was the anointed one of God?

Joseph and Mary were Jews and kept strictly to the Jewish religious laws. On the eighth day after Jesus was born he was circumcised and given the name 'Jesus' just as the angel had instructed. After forty days he was taken to the temple in Jerusalem where various ceremonies were performed because Jesus was the first-born male of the family.[12]

Surely it would be here at the great temple in Jerusalem which had taken King Herod ten years to build and which was the main centre for the Jewish religion, that an angel from God would dramatically reveal to the Jewish leaders who Jesus was? But no angel came. And the religious leaders ignored this simple working-class family from the north, an area which was despised because the Jews there had mixed more with their neighbours from other races.

Instead, it was two white-haired old people who recognized who Jesus really was as he was carried by his parents into the temple. Wisdom that comes with age and the living of a righteous life enabled these people to see what the religious authorities could not see. One of the old people was a man called Simeon, the other a woman aged more than eighty-four called Anna. God had revealed to Simeon that he would not die until he had seen 'the anointed one' — the Messiah. As the venerable old man held Jesus in his arms, he praised God with some remarkable words:

> Sovereign Lord, as you have promised,
> you now dismiss your servant in peace.
> For my eyes have seen your salvation,
> which you have prepared in the sight of all people,
> a light for revelation to the Gentiles
> and for the glory of your people Israel.[13]

Simeon *knew* that here in his arms was the one that God had promised. All he wanted to do now was to die in peace. As he looked at that tiny baby he *knew* that in his arms was the one who would bring the salvation God was preparing for his people. Not only was this salvation going to bless his own people, the Jews, but it was also going to be a light to the 'Gentiles', the word used in the Bible to describe all the other nations of the world. For a frail old man, about to die, it was a remarkable prophecy to make about a tiny baby, a child of an unknown carpenter coming from the most despised area of a tiny state which was still under military occupation.

Meanwhile, the old prophetess called Anna started telling anyone who was 'looking forward to the redemption of Jerusalem' about the significance of this child, Jesus.[14] What did she mean? Was Jesus destined to join the Zealots and deliver Jerusalem from the grip of Roman rule?

Within a year or two, Jesus' presence in Bethlehem came to the attention of the authorities. A group of 'magi' arrived from some country to the east. The term 'magi' was used by the historian Herodotus to refer to a tribe of the Medes who had a priestly function in the Persian Empire. But it also had a more general meaning of 'wise men' or the 'astrologers' who interpreted the meanings of events and studied the stars. The group of magi who arrived in Jerusalem had probably been travelling for some months and must have caused quite a stir as they arrived in the city. But the greatest stir was caused by the question they were asking, 'Where is the one who has been born king of the Jews? We saw his star in the east and have come to worship him.'[15]

It is hardly surprising that King Herod was greatly disturbed when he heard of their investigations. King of the Jews? Why, everyone knew that he had been king of the Jews for nearly forty years! He was a loyal friend of the Romans. Had he not put down

vigorously all opposition to Roman imperialism? He was not
going to allow a few astrologers to stir up any trouble with the
people.

Carefully Herod inquired from the Jewish religious leaders in
Jerusalem where the Messiah was going to be born. Their reply
was quite clear. Anyone who had studied the Old Testament
thoroughly knew that the Messiah was going to be born in Bethlehem.[16] Ironically it was therefore Herod himself who sent the
magi off down the road to Bethlehem. There the star that they
had seen in the east stopped right over the home where Jesus was
staying.

What was this star? Did it have anything to do with the con-
junction of Jupiter and Saturn which took place in 7 BC? Or with
the evanescent star of 4 BC mentioned in ancient Chinese records?
Probably we will never know. But the whole point of the story is
not the nature of the star but the direction in which it was
pointing. As the group of magi finally arrived at the home of
Joseph's relatives, they saw the child Jesus with his mother Mary
and presented precious gifts of gold, incense and myrrh, a sweet-
smelling resin widely used in cosmetics as well as in various religious rites of those times. Then, without telling Herod, the magi
returned quietly to the east by another route.

So it was non-Jews who were the very first ones to show respect
to Jesus and present him with gifts — not the local religious
leaders. The words of Simeon seemed to be coming true sooner
than anyone had expected.

Dramatic events quickly overtook Joseph's family. King
Herod was furious at the thought that a rival king might be growing up in neighbouring Bethlehem. Why, it was not even the
capital city! We know from other historical sources how
threatened Herod felt by opposition to his own position. In fact
he even had three of his own sons executed upon suspicion that
they were plotting against him.

Soon after the magi had left, an angel appeared to Joseph in a
dream and told him to take his family quickly to Egypt to escape
Herod's wrath.[17] That night Joseph and Mary set out with Jesus
on the long journey down to Egypt. So one of the very earliest
experiences of the young child Jesus was that of being a refugee.
Where they stayed and what they did in Egypt we are not told.

What we do know is that after Joseph and his family had fled, King Herod had all the boys in Bethlehem less than two years old brutally killed so that there would be no further threat to his throne.[18]

Soon after this savage massacre King Herod died. God then told Joseph through an angel in a dream that it was now safe for them to return to their homeland. So Joseph brought the family back to live in Mary's home town of Nazareth.

Jesus grows up

Very little is known about the childhood of Jesus. Some people find this surprising. Surely, they say, in the biographies of such a famous man we should find some details of what he ate and drank, of the clothes he wore, of some of his childhood experiences. But of all this we know nothing. We do not even know whether Jesus was ugly or handsome. Any pictures that you might see are based entirely on the artist's own imagination.

Why this silence? The Gospel-writers are not in fact biographers in the modern sense of that term. They are deliberately selective. They purposely focus on those parts of the life of Jesus which will help us to understand who he really was and why he came. The spotlight is placed on two key times in the life of Jesus — the events surrounding his birth which we have just been considering, and the last three years of his life which we are about to consider. Of the intervening thirty years, we are told almost nothing.

Why? The reason is simple. The Gospel-writers do not want us to be distracted from the main point. Perhaps if we knew what hairstyle Jesus had there would be those who would insist that his followers looked alike. The same would probably be true if we knew what clothes he wore. But all these points would be tangents — lines into space leading us away from the central point. They would quickly become fog shrouding the true nature of his mission, making it more difficult to understand. So the Gospel-writers prune away this distracting material and give us instead what we really need to know — the very heart of the message about Jesus. People who wrote much later on about

Jesus, in the second century, tried to add many speculative stories about his childhood experiences. But these stories have no historical basis and are not worth taking seriously. As time passes, all kinds of stories grow up around famous people who have died, stories which are often passed on and believed by later generations. That is why it is so important to listen to those who knew Jesus personally and lived with him over a period of several years.

There is just one point mentioned about Jesus as a child. He was extraordinarily wise for his age: God's blessing was on him.[19] This wisdom is illustrated by an incident which took place when Jesus was twelve years old.[20] He was taken by his parents to one of the Jewish feasts in Jerusalem. On the way back to Nazareth Mary and Joseph found that Jesus was missing from their group. They returned to Jerusalem and finally found the boy in the temple discussing important questions with the religious leaders there. Astonished, they asked Jesus what he was doing. His reply gives us an important clue: 'Didn't you know I had to be in my father's house?'

We read that Joseph and Mary did not understand what he was saying, so we should not be surprised if we fail to understand immediately the meaning of those words. For the parents of Jesus, as for the others listening, it was to be more than eighteen years before the full shocking significance of that short conversation hit them.

1   Matthew 2:1
2   Luke 2:1
3   Luke 2:4
4   Matthew 1:19
5   Matthew 1:20
6   Matthew 1:21
7   Luke 1:26–38
8   Luke 22:11
9   Luke 2:7
10 Luke 2:8–20
11 Luke 2:17–18
12 Luke 2:22–24
13 Luke 2:29–32

14 Luke 2:36–38
15 Matthew 2:1–2
16 Matthew 2:3–6; see also John 7:42
17 Matthew 2:13
18 Matthew 2:16
19 Luke 2:40
20 Luke 2:41–52

The Beginning of Jesus' Public Life

Jesus worked in the family carpentry business in Nazareth until the age of about thirty. In fact the word used for 'carpenter' in the Gospels has the more general meaning of 'builder', and probably Jesus was involved in building projects as well as making things such as agricultural tools and furniture. It was a tough life that involved much hard work. Economically it would have been made even harder by the heavy tax demanded by the Roman authorities. By his late twenties Jesus would have known all about the economic and cultural imperialism of Rome, and the poorer section of the community's sheer battle to survive as they faced times of drought and the terrible grip of the money-lenders.

What suddenly changed Jesus from a worker in a small provincial town into being a great religious leader? Why did he give up a safe job to take to the road with a small band of followers?

John the Baptist

We cannot understand the beginning of Jesus' public life without taking a look at John the Baptist, who is given this title to distinguish him from a follower of Jesus also called John who wrote one of the Gospels.

John the Baptist was a relative of Jesus. He was born shortly before Jesus and some remarkable events were associated with his birth too.[1] But there the similarities end. Far from being a typical working man as Jesus was, John the Baptist was brought up in the desert. There he lived an ascetic life of self-denial which was more typical of the prophets that God had sent in previous centuries.[2]

Some people think that John the Baptist may have had contact with the Essenes, a Jewish sect who practised community life. The Essenes had a centre at Qumran near the north-west of the Dead Sea. This is where the famous Dead Sea Scrolls were discovered in 1947. These are a collection of ancient manuscripts which include the writings of the Essenes as well as some parts of the Bible.

It is quite possible that John the Baptist did indeed have contact with the Essenes, but the message that he started preaching in the desert was quite distinct from the teachings of the Essene community. They taught that the only way to practise the laws of Moses properly was to live an ascetic life well away from the world, whereas John taught that people should truly practise God's laws right in the midst of their everyday secular lives. Far from encouraging people to live in the desert, away from the world, John taught them that God wanted to change their lives right where they were.[3]

The central theme of John's message was that he was coming to prepare the way for Jesus. There were two main parts to this preparation. One was to call the people back to a true obedience to God's law. This involved turning away from evil, 'repentance'. This change of heart was vividly symbolized by baptism — immersing people in the River Jordan nearby. The word 'baptism' comes from a Greek word which means 'to dip'. The word was used for the washing of hands in water, or the dyeing of clothes as they were immersed in a bath. Going into the water during baptism was a dramatic picture of an inward change in direction in the person's life and heart. John emphasized that such repentance had no meaning unless it resulted in definite changes in the person's life.[4]

The second part of John the Baptist's preparation campaign was to point away from himself to Jesus as the one that the people should follow. Some people thought that John the Baptist himself was the Messiah.[5] But John constantly denied this and pointed to Jesus.[6] Indeed he said some extraordinary things about Jesus. He claimed that while he was baptizing them with water only, Jesus was actually going to 'baptize' or 'immerse' them in God's Holy Spirit. Furthermore, when John saw Jesus one day he pointed at him and said, 'Look, the Lamb of God, who takes away the sin of the world!'[7]

Since most of John's hearers would have been Jews, there is only one meaning that they could possibly have understood from these words. They would immediately have thought of the lambs which were frequently used as sacrifice for sin in Jewish festivals. The most famous festival of all was called the Passover feast. Held once a year, this festival was a way of remembering the time when the Jews were freed from slavery. At the heart of the festival was the sacrifice of a lamb. The death due to the person because of his sin was symbolically transferred to the animal. In the same way in many countries today lambs are frequently used as animal sacrifices.

The people listening to John the Baptist must have understood that he was saying Jesus was to be some kind of sacrifice — with the extraordinary claim that it was to be a sacrifice for the sin of the whole world! Had the desert sun driven John the Baptist mad?

Many people thought that the long-awaited Messiah — the great Saviour — was going to come as a conquering king or as a revolutionary hero. Above all, this hero would deliver the Jews from all their oppressors. So what was this talk about the 'whole world'? And how could the picture of a 'lamb' possibly fit with the idea of a triumphant king? A lamb was innocent and helpless.

The baptism of Jesus

The crucial moment in the work of John the Baptist came when Jesus himself was baptized in the River Jordan. Not surprisingly John the Baptist at first refused to baptize Jesus.[8] How could he baptize the very one for whom he was preparing the way? And what did Jesus have to repent of anyway? Yet Jesus insisted. He said that he had to be baptized 'to do all that God requires'.[9]

It is crucial to understand the meaning of the baptism of Jesus. If you miss what happened there, then you may miss the significance of the whole of the rest of his life.

When Jesus was baptized, it was an act of identification with the suffering human race. By a conscious act of the will he was beginning to take the sinner's place. Though he had nothing to repent of, yet he gladly stood where a repentant sinner stood.

And it was at this moment of dramatic obedience to God's will that the heaven was opened and God's Spirit descended on Jesus like a dove. Why a dove? It was a dove that first brought news back to Noah in the ark that the flood waters were receding, by plucking and bringing a leaf from a newly-grown tree. What a picture of deliverance from death as the flood waters receded! It was a dove that was offered as a sin-offering in certain Jewish ceremonies. In many countries of the world today the white dove is still a symbol of peace and deliverance, and doves are released on occasions of great rejoicing such as weddings. Perhaps the dove on the day of Jesus' baptism had all these meanings and more, but the main point is that heaven opened and God's Spirit descended on Jesus. What does this mean?

It means that Jesus had the full blessing and power of God to carry out the work for which he had come. It means that Jesus was just like 'the servant of the Lord' about whom Isaiah the prophet had spoken 800 years before when he wrote:

> Here is my servant, whom I uphold,
> my chosen one in whom I delight;
> I will put my Spirit on him
> and he will bring justice to the nations.[10]

God's Spirit coming upon Jesus was both a sign and a seal of God's approval as Jesus took the place of a servant by standing in the River Jordan.

To leave no shadow of doubt about the crucial significance of this event, a voice came from heaven: 'This is my Son, whom I love; with him I am well pleased.'[11]

Some people say that they are willing to read the New Testament because of the high moral ideals which it teaches, but that they do not like the Old Testament because it is too long and boring. But we will never fully understand the New without also reading the Old. The New Testament is full of quotations, pictures and examples from the Old. The voice from heaven quoted from the Old Testament.

The fact that a voice came from heaven at all is extraordinary. For the Jews the heavens had been silent for a very long time. When God spoke he spoke by his Holy Spirit. But many Jewish leaders believed that the Holy Spirit had departed from Israel after the last of the true prophets with whose writings the Old Testament closes. This is why there is a historical gap of several hundred years between the close of the Old Testament and the start of the New during which God did not speak to his people because of their disobedience and sin.

But here to people's amazement was the real thing again! God was speaking once more from heaven.

The words 'This is my Son' are a quotation from Psalm 2:7. In its original context this psalm is about the kings of ancient Israel. By the time of Jesus it was widely seen as a prediction of the character of the coming Messiah. The psalm is about the power and the majesty of the son of the king that God appoints, and the impossibility of standing against such a man. Yes, surely the Messiah will be like that? There was no Jew burdened by the tax of imperial Rome who did not look forward to *that* kind of deliverance.

But what was the rest of the sentence spoken from heaven? It is a phrase from the verse in Isaiah 42:1 which we have quoted above. There the whole passage is about God's chosen one being like a servant. It was upon such a servant that God would place his Spirit. The servant would come humbly and gently to fulfil God's plan — very far from powerful images of kingship.[12] Most Jews certainly did not see this passage as referring to the coming Messiah. How could such a picture of the humble servant fit with the more popular idea of the conquering king? But the voice from heaven was insistent; tear these two ideas apart and you will never understand who Jesus is. The Messiah is to be both a king and a servant.

The temptation of Jesus

Immediately after Jesus was baptized, he was tempted by the devil, called Satan, for a period of forty days during a time of prayer and fasting in the desert. Once you understand what the voice from heaven was really saying at the baptism of Jesus, then you will be able to appreciate the crucial significance of these temptations.

Satan's tempting of Jesus centred on one main point — the attempt to persuade Jesus to concentrate on his kingly power and forget his role of a servant. Satan knew that if this happened then Jesus' whole work on earth would in fact be finished and wasted.

In his very first temptation, Satan tried to make Jesus turn stones into bread.[13] He would have been desperately hungry after his fast of forty days without food. Satan came to Jesus and in effect said: 'Come on, be a superman! Use your power to save yourself and satisfy your own desires! Isn't that what being a king is all about?' But Jesus refused.

Then Satan tried to get Jesus to leap off the top of the great temple at Jerusalem. What a dramatic moment it would be as he floated to earth, unharmed! How the people would hail him as king as soon as they realized he had supernatural powers! Once again Jesus drove home his refusal with some blunt words from the Old Testament.[14]

Another trick Satan tried was to pretend that the final authority over the world was actually in *his* hands. He told Jesus that he would give him authority over all the 'kingdoms of the world' if only he would bow down and worship him.[15] This was the ultimate lie. People today are tempted in a similar way when they are encouraged to contact the spirits of dead people and tap evil powers. What they do not realize (until it is too late) is that the power they tap finally becomes their master. Jesus responded with another simple but profound quote from the Old Testament: 'Worship the Lord your God and serve him only.'

It is worth looking up the original story of the fall of mankind. You will find it in the first few pages of the Bible, in Genesis 3:1–7. Some people think that this story is an interesting ancient myth but has little relevance for us now. But here in this simple yet profound account we are given the key to why we find ourselves in such a terrible mess today, with enormous stockpiles of nuclear weapons ready to blow the world to bits, with so much money being spent on defence that nations can hardly feed their own people and with imperialism extending to the most distant places. The story in Genesis tells us how at the beginning man and woman decided that they wished to be like God. They wanted to grab the power and knowledge that God had clearly said they should *not* possess. They wanted to listen to Satan's words and not God's, and put themselves in centre-stage. Ever since, people have gone on being little tin gods, with terrible results.

When people decided to disobey God, a cancerous alienation came into the world which had not been there before. It was an alienation between mankind and God, between mankind and his fellows, between mankind and himself. It is not for nothing that many languages have the expression: 'He was his own worst enemy . . .'

We now know that the physical cause of many cancers is the wrong control of 'oncogenes' in our genetic material. An oncogene is a small gene which, when over-activated, can cause cancer. At the fall of man it was as if a spiritual 'oncogene' of alienation came into the human race and spread with terrifying results. The root of the 'oncogene' was man's ridiculous belief that the world was his and that he could do with it just as he liked.

There is a close similarity between the temptations of Jesus and the fall of man. Satan's temptations of Jesus in the desert were like a replay of his testings of man back at the beginning. It was like playing the same old video through again, but this time with different actors — and a different ending. Satan wanted to catch Jesus in the same selfish trap of self-centred power-seeking with which he had caught the rest of the human race. But Jesus refused to be caught. In fact he was the first person who ever lived who was not caught in this trap. In that dramatic struggle in the wilderness with satanic powers, he fought the devil and won. He refused to bow to Satan because the whole goal of his life was true submission to God. He refused to allow his kingly powers to be used for selfish ends. He refused to separate the fact of his kingship from the fact of his being a servant.

Jesus calls the twelve disciples

The word 'disciple' means 'learner' or 'pupil'. In the time of Jesus, as today in many parts of the world, it was very common for well-known teachers to gather around them a group of apprentices or learners. This was as true for Greek philosophers as it was for Jewish rabbis. The best-known teachers would, of course, try to gather around them a group of gifted and intelligent disciples who would best reflect their master's capabilities.

So in comparison it is a shock to look at the twelve disciples that Jesus personally chose! We find a list of their names in Mark 3:13–19. There were at least four fishermen in the group, probably more. One, called Matthew, was from those highly-distrusted members of society, the tax-collectors. Simon the Zealot, as mentioned before, may have been involved in a nationalistic activist group concerned with overthrowing Roman power. Judas Iscariot was appointed treasurer for the group, but ended up stealing from the money-bag. Later on he was the one who betrayed Jesus.

What a bunch of people with which to start a spiritual revolution! But is that not just the point? Jesus deliberately chose a typical cross-section of his society. Since his home was near the Sea of Galilee, naturally fishing, the main industry of the area, would be well represented. The fishermen of the area were rough, tough, conservative and very loyal. Later on Jesus nicknamed two of them who were brothers 'sons of thunder' because they were so impetuous! They were totally different from the smooth-tongued tax-collectors and the politically-minded Zealots. As far as we know Jesus did not even include any of the Jewish religious elite in his group. He was more interested in the lives of ordinary people.

He started with just twelve — living with them, travelling with them, sharing his daily life with them. Though Jesus could speak and read Hebrew, they spoke Aramaic together, the normal daily language of the Jewish people, keeping Greek for their contact with the non-Jewish people of the area.

With these twelve very ordinary men, so full of the weaknesses and failings which face us all, Jesus began to demonstrate in daily life that his kingship was not some lofty religious ideal for the future life, but a daily practical reality. God's kingdom was about to break into the world of fallen people right before their eyes.

1 Luke 1:5–80
2 Matthew 3:4
3 Luke 3:10–14
4 Luke 3:8

5   Luke 3:15
6   Matthew 3:11–12
7   John 1:29
8   Matthew 3:14
9   Matthew 3:15
10 Isaiah 42:1
11 Matthew 3:17
12 Isaiah 42:1–4
13 Luke 4:3
14 Luke 4:12
15 Luke 4:5–7
16 Luke 4:8

Jesus and the Kingdom of God

The kingdom of God is at the heart of the teaching of Jesus. As soon as Jesus had chosen his first disciples, he went throughout his home district of Galilee 'preaching the good news of the kingdom.'[1]

But what does that really mean? Was Jesus trying to establish some religious state on earth? Or was he talking about some future kingdom in heaven?

Most people today live in countries which do not have kings. And even if we do, it may not help us understand what Jesus is saying.

What helps more is to look at the original word for 'kingdom' in the New Testament. The Greek word is *basileia*. It refers to the rank, authority and sovereignty which a king possesses. In the Old Testament, the equivalent Hebrew word is *malkuth*, which has the same root as the old Turkish *melekut* and the Arabic *mamlakatun*. It means the same — the dominion and power of the king.

So when Jesus refers to the 'kingdom of God', he is not talking about a geographical area, but about the reign and authority of God. This becomes clear when we consider a well-known story that Jesus told about the kingdom of God.[2] The story is about a man of noble birth who goes off to a distant country to have himself appointed king, and then returns. In the original Greek it says that the man 'went to receive the *basileia* (the kingdom)'. Obviously he was not going to fetch a piece of land and bring it home with him! The land was already there. He was a man of noble birth. What he needed was the authority (the *basileia*) to rule over a certain area.

There was a local historical example which the people listening to Jesus would probably have remembered. In 40 BC political conditions in Palestine had become very chaotic. The Romans had been trying to subdue the area, but with limited success. Finally Herod the Great went to Rome, obtained from the Roman Senate the *basileia*, the kingdom, and returned to Palestine to exercise his newly-gained kingly authority.

As Jesus passionately began to proclaim that 'the kingdom of God is at hand', this was not some new theory about life after death, but a declaration of God's dynamic power and authority right there and then on earth. God had not sent a prophet for hundreds of years due to the disobedience of the people. But now something totally new was about to happen. God's reign was about to break into the world in a way that it had never done before.

The dynamic of the kingdom

It was not long before people found that the words of Jesus about the 'kingdom' were no mere talk. People who were ill were made well again. Lepers were healed of their terrible skin disease. Demons were cast out. The dead were restored to life. And Jesus made it perfectly clear that all of this was due to God's kingly authority.[3]

But Jesus was not just another wonder-worker, intent on drawing the crowds. His miracles flowed from compassion. The dynamic of the kingdom was the dynamic of love.

Nowhere is this more seen than in the attitude that Jesus showed towards lepers. The lepers of the day were viewed by society as the lowest of the low. They had to ring a bell as they walked down the street to warn people that they were coming. Everyone was terrified to touch them because of the fear of catching the disease. Most people thought that God must be punishing a leper because of some sin committed by him or by his family.

Very early on in the public ministry of Jesus, a leper came and fell at his feet. If this had happened to any of the religious leaders of the day, they would have screamed for someone to come and drag the leper away before their 'holy' body was made unclean by the contact. But Jesus did no such thing. As the man pleaded for healing, Jesus was filled with compassion for him. Reaching out his hand, he *touched* the leper and said 'Be clean.' Immediately the leper was healed. There was no big crowd, no noise, no fuss — just the quiet word of authority.

Jesus was not like some so-called 'faith healers' of today, who can only 'heal' with big crowds and mass excitement (making psychosomatic cures more likely by group suggestion), and whose egos are matched only by the size of their collection plates. Jesus simply spoke, and it happened. In fact, in this case he was so concerned to avoid the wrong kind of publicity that he strictly warned the man not to tell anyone — though, hardly surprisingly, the man was unable to keep the good news to himself and went around telling everybody![5]

Jesus did not just talk about compassion — he lived it. Unfortunately today there are many religious leaders who talk a lot about love and compassion, but that is as far as it goes. It is meaningless to talk about the compassion of God unless we ourselves are willing to be involved with the needs of others.

Yet Jesus never forced his compassion on people. There had to be the human response. There had to be the willingness to receive what God was longing to give. This is nowhere more clearly seen than in the story of the paralyzed man who used to lie beside the pool of Bethesda.[6]

The pool of Bethesda was well known in first-century Jerusalem. It was surrounded by five covered areas supported by pillars. Crowds of sick people used to gather in these areas around the pool every day, because there was a local legend that, when the water became stirred up, the first sick person into the water would be healed.

One day Jesus went to visit the pool and saw a sick man lying there on his mat. On inquiry, Jesus discovered that he had been an invalid for no less than thirty-eight years. Then Jesus asked him a question which, on the face of it, seems quite extraordinary.

'Do you want to get well?' he asked the man.

I work in a hospital. Imagine that I go up to a very sick patient, who perhaps has been lying in the hospital for thirty-eight days, not thirty-eight years, who is in pain and is paying out enormous sums of money for his hospital treatment, and I ask him, 'Do you want to get well?' The patient might perhaps be excused for thinking that I was a little strange!

But there is something very perceptive and important in the question that Jesus asked the man at the pool of Bethesda. He could no doubt see that this man was in a complete rut. If you do the same thing for thirty-eight years, then you are very likely to get in a rut. Did this man really *want* to get better? That was the question.

Probably the man knew everyone at the pool. This was his daily routine, his social life, his community. Like a man who has been so long in prison he can no longer imagine being free, the man had to be ready to be set free from more than the prison-like bars of his physical paralysis. So Jesus asked him 'Do you *want* to get well?' The man's reply must have indicated to Jesus that he had at least enough desire for the next crucial step. Jesus commanded 'Get up! Pick up your mat and walk'. Just like the leper, the man was immediately cured, and he picked up his mat and walked. The man had no idea who Jesus was. As for Jesus, he slipped away into the crowd to avoid unnecessary publicity.[7]

The kingdom of God cannot be forced on anyone. There has to be that openness to God to allow him to make us whole people. He will never force his way into our lives.

In fact we are all like that man at the pool of Bethesda in some way or other. We have habits in our lives that need changing. But we cling onto them. They have become part of us and we feel threatened to let them go. Sometimes these things are more than mere habits. Like hatred, for example. Some people hold a deep hatred in their hearts for another person, family or community — perhaps for something that was done years ago against them, and the fires of revenge are still burning on inside them. Hatred is a great destroyer, not of the one who is hated but of the one who hates. The question of Jesus remains the same: 'Do you want to get well?'

There were some people for whose agreement Jesus did not wait before demonstrating the power of God's kingdom in their lives. These were the people whose lives were so possessed by demons that they no longer had control over their own destiny. Jesus went straight to the real source of their problems and confronted the demonic powers directly.

Here perhaps more than anywhere else in the ministry of Jesus we see a direct and dramatic confrontation between the kingdom of darkness and the kingdom of light. The demons themselves often recognized his kingly authority and shouted in fear as they realized who Jesus was.

For example, there was the man in Capernaum possessed by an evil spirit who cried out as he saw Jesus: 'What do you want with us, Jesus of Nazareth? Have you come to destroy us? I know who you are — the Holy One of God!'

'Be quiet!' said Jesus sternly. 'Come out of him!'

The evil spirit shook the man violently and came out of him with a shriek.

The very same evening Jesus drove out many more demons, but he would not let the demons speak because they knew who he was.[9]

Perhaps the most dramatic instance was when Jesus met a man filled with evil spirits on the shores of the Sea of Galilee.[10] This man lived among the tombs. People had often tried to chain him to control his violent outbursts, but each time he had broken loose. He went around the area screaming and cutting himself with stones.

As Jesus directly confronted the evil spirits in the man, they begged to be left alone, recognizing clearly the authority that he possessed.[11] But Jesus would have none of it. He cast out the many demons possessing the man and let them enter a herd of pigs nearby. The herd, about 2,000 in number, rushed down the steep bank into the lake and were drowned. What more vivid proof did the man need that the evil spirits had really been driven out? And what was the value of a herd of pigs (forbidden in Jewish religion in any case) compared to the worth of a single human being? In this single act, Jesus restored both the man's sanity and his self-respect. But he refused to let the man follow him — his first responsibility was to go and be with his family.[12]

If you come from the darkness of the night into a brightly-lit room, the light seems to be blinding. So it must have seemed to those evil powers as they were faced with the blinding light of God's kingdom. There is nothing like the bright beam of a searchlight to emphasize the intense blackness of the darkness around.

Millions of people in the world today are in the grip of the devil's power. They may not be possessed by evil spirits, but they certainly live in fear and bondage to evil, satanic powers. They read horoscopes and even try to plan their lives by what they read. Others visit mediums to try to obtain secret powers which will help them gain control over their enemies or over their own destinies. Through amulets and charms, special prayers and verses from religious books to be worn around the neck, ouija boards and tarot cards, seances and psychics, a network of fear is built around people's lives. This fear comes from Satan, it does not come from God.

Jesus came to proclaim deliverance from all satanic powers. With his coming, God's kingdom broke into the world to clash with the powers of darkness. A new age was about to begin.

As the community of Jesus' followers came into being — first of the twelve disciples and then of a wider circle of seventy — so they too were given authority by Jesus to 'heal the sick, raise the dead, cleanse lepers, cast out demons, saying "the kingdom of heaven is at hand." '[13] It was as if a stone had been dropped in a pond, and now the ripples of the kingdom were beginning to spread out in all directions. At the beginning, the ripples were restricted to a very small area — Galilee and the surrounding districts. But it was not many years before news of the kingdom reached Rome itself, the capital of the mighty Roman Empire — and then the world beyond.

The ethics of the kingdom

It is very easy for power to become divorced from morality. But the last thing Jesus was interested in was naked power. Whenever he sensed that crowds of people were following him just because he had done some miracles, he would turn around and say some very tough words to them.[14] For those who realized that God's kingdom was truly breaking in upon them, there was only one logical thing to do — repent![15] Turn away from the old life of evil! Turn towards God's new kingdom-life of love and holiness.

Jesus summarized his teaching on the ethics of God's kingdom in his famous 'Sermon on the Mount'.[16] Read the chapters containing the sermon if you wish to find the essence of Jesus' teaching.

In this sermon, Jesus hammered home the message that submission to the reign of God goes far beyond the mere practice of certain religious rituals. God's laws demand nothing less than perfection for the person who really wants to follow him. And we can only start on the path to perfection by first realizing our own spiritual bankruptcy and inability to achieve perfection by our own strength.

Right at the beginning of his sermon, Jesus proclaimed: 'Blessed are the poor in spirit, for theirs is the kingdom of heaven.'[17]

Jesus is not talking about the physically poor, though poor people may be more likely than the rich to understand the real point of his message. Rather, Jesus is saying here that the kingdom of heaven belongs to those who realize that their own human resources are totally inadequate as a means of entering God's kingdom. In this one simple phrase lies the death of religion. Religion involves *us* in doing something in order to try to please God. When we have obeyed the laws of religion, when we have done all that we were told to do, then we feel self-satisfied — we believe that we have done all that God requires of us. Jesus gave us the Sermon on the Mount to shatter our complacency and to show us that the ethics of the kingdom of God demand perfection and nothing less.

The religious leaders at the time of Jesus were very concerned with the outward details of religious observance. But Jesus forced them to look inwards into the inner recesses of their own hearts. The essence of God's law was not in rituals but in reality, not in outward religiosity but in inward revolution.

So, said Jesus, anger against another person is really like murder in the sight of God.[18] We kill with our hearts. Judicially and socially, anger and murder are of course different. But God understands our innermost motives. The demands of his kingdom go way beyond outward adherence to the law.

The same is true when it comes to sexual lust. Adultery, Jesus taught, is not just in the act, but in the lustful thoughts which occur in our minds.[19] Again, judicially and socially, adultery has different consequences from lust. But the kingdom of God is a kingdom which challenges us with total submission to God of our whole beings, including our mind, will and conscience. Anything less than that is not real submission at all.

Jesus even said that we should love our enemies and pray for those who persecute us!

'If you love those who love you, what reward will you get? . . . And if you greet only your brothers, what are you doing more than others? Do not even pagans do that? Be perfect, therefore, as your heavenly Father is perfect.'[20]

At this point we may protest: 'But this is impossible! Surely these beautiful but impractical ideas must be for some future heavenly state? God cannot possibly expect us to live them out in the present evil age. Who can practise such teachings?'

The answer is — no one can, at least not in our own strength. The demands of God's kingdom are always far beyond us, just as the holiness of God is always far above us. This is why the opening statement of Jesus' sermon is so important — until we realize our own spiritual poverty, there is no way that we can belong to the kingdom of heaven. We cannot even begin on God's true path.

But these kingdom ethics are certainly for the present time in which we live, not just for some future 'golden age'. Jesus was speaking to people oppressed by imperial Rome. He, like them, knew all about the greed, deceit and lust for power which goes along with imperialism. And as he preached the ethics of God's kingdom, he was preaching a message which was ultimately going to be more subversive than the most revolutionary political philosophies.

The seed of the kingdom

Having just talked about the revolutionary nature of God's kingdom, it may seem rather curious to be talking in the next breath about the 'seed of the kingdom'. But that is just how Jesus talked about it. He once likened the kingdom of God to a tiny grain of mustard seed, a seed so small that it can hardly be seen lying in the palm of the hand.[21] But when the seed grows, it becomes a large plant.

What is Jesus saying here? Simply this — that God's kingdom begins in small ways but ends up big. To underline this point, Jesus immediately told another story, saying that the kingdom is like yeast being mixed with dough.[22] It only takes a handful of yeast to make a very large amount of bread. Again the picture is of something small and apparently insignificant which ends up exerting an influence out of all proportion to its initial size.

If the reign of God was so powerful and the ethics of the kingdom so revolutionary, why was there any opposition to the teachings of Jesus? Why did God not simply stop all the evil and wars right then, finish with all the people who were not obeying his laws, and set up a new kingdom on earth consisting of those who wished to obey him?

The answer is in the seed. Before a seed can germinate, it has to fall into the ground and be hidden from sight. Once germination has taken place, a new shoot then has to push its way up through the soil before it finally appears. The reign of God begins in a quiet way in people's hearts as they willingly submit their lives to him. Then they join with others who are also on the same path of submission and a community is formed. It is a community of loving response, not of forceful coercion. But it all takes time.

Biological systems teach us that time is important in order for significant changes to occur. The rhythm of the seasons, the growth of the infant, springtime and harvest — we are part of a creation in which abrupt changes are often counter-productive. When they do occur, they tend to be called 'catastrophes'. Although the kingdom of God may break into someone's life with dramatic power at the beginning, the real fruit — the ethics of God's kingdom — take time to appear.

Once some of the Jewish leaders from the sect of the Pharisees asked Jesus when the kingdom of God would come.[23]

Jesus replied: 'The kingdom of God does not come visibly, nor will people say, "Here it is," or "There it is," because the kingdom of God is within you.'

Of course there were many people listening to Jesus who were longing for political revolution. They wanted Jesus to be a political Messiah who would overthrow Rome and release Palestine from its grip. But he refused to allow people to make him into that kind of king — a mere rival king to the emperor of Rome.[24]

God's kingdom was a universal kingdom, not restricted to any particular group of people.

So Jesus told his listeners that 'the kingdom of God is within you'. It is not something that is going to happen only in the future, but something that is to happen inside us right now. We are responsible for our own destinies and for the destinies of those around us. We cannot fatalistically postpone the solutions to all our problems to some future heavenly age when God will act in power. God *is* acting in power right now, and we are responsible to respond to that power. 'The kingdom of God is *within* you' — that was the message of Jesus.

There was a tension in his teachings, too, on this point. If you read the New Testament you will find some places in which Jesus refers to the present reality of the kingdom, and some where he refers to the future reality. They are two aspects at two different times of the same truth.

Imagine that you are in a pleasant garden with a very high wall. It is full of beautiful flowers and trees, but there are ugly things in it too — nasty weeds which threaten to strangle the flowers, big black slugs which nibble the fresh green of the leaves, and the persistent smell of death and decay which spoils the fresh smell of the blossoms. Then suddenly a large door opens in the wall at the end of the garden. Through the door you catch a glimpse of blinding light, a light so bright that it makes the sunshine in your garden look grey by comparison. And just visible in the midst of the light is a garden so perfect, with a profusion of colours so vivid and a mass of trees so green, that again it makes your garden look quite drab. Suddenly a warm breeze, heavily-laden with the smell of nectar, wafts into your garden from the garden beyond. The breeze carries with it not only heavenly smells, but also a flurry of seeds and pollen which scatter all over your garden, sowing new life, colour and power among the weeds and slugs. The door closes again, but things will never be the same again. Part of the future has come into the present, and from those seeds will come a harvest.

The cost of the kingdom

On many occasions Jesus hammered home to his listeners the point that the kingdom of God was only for those who would seek it wholeheartedly. He said that the kingdom was like a treasure hidden in a field. When someone found the treasure he went and sold all that he had so that he could buy the field.[25]

The kingdom must come first in our hearts, said Jesus. If we seek it first, then all the other daily necessities of life will be provided.[26] But if we spend all our time worrying about food and clothing, then the priorities of the kingdom will be squeezed out.

Jesus also taught that it was hard for rich people to enter the kingdom.[27] In fact he said that 'it is easier for a camel to go through the eye of a needle than for a rich man to enter the kingdom of God.'[28] In other words it takes a special miracle for a rich person to accept God's reign in his life — not because there is something wrong with the riches themselves, but because the riches are so likely to have a hold on the person's heart that he will find it difficult to allow control of them to go to another. Jesus said that we cannot serve two masters.[29] We cannot both serve God and allow our lives to be dominated by a love for money. God's kingdom demands all that we have and all that we are.

Once we submit to God's reign, then there is no going back. 'No one who puts his hand to the plough and looks back,' said Jesus, 'is fit for service in the kingdom of God.'[30]

1   Matthew 4:23
2   Luke 19:11–27
3   Matthew 4:23; 12:38
4   Mark 1:40–45
5   Mark 1:45
6   John 5:1–9
7   John 5:13
8   Mark 1:23–27
9   Mark 1:32–34
10 Mark 5:1–20
11 Mark 5:7–8
12 Mark 5:19

13 Matthew 10:7; Luke 10:9
14 Luke 11:29–32
15 Matthew 4:17
16 Matthew 5 – 7. Note that in Matthew's Gospel the term 'the
    kingdom of heaven' is used rather than 'the kingdom of
    God'. This is because Matthew was writing especially for a
    Jewish readership. For the strict Jews, it was blasphemous
    even to mention the name of 'God', so Matthew translates
    the 'kingdom of God' as the 'kingdom of heaven'. The
    meaning of the two phrases is identical.
17 Matthew 5:3
18 Matthew 5:21–22
19 Matthew 5:27–28
20 Matthew 5:46–48
21 Matthew 13:31–32
22 Matthew 13:33
23 Luke 17:20–21
24 John 6:15
25 Matthew 13:44
26 Matthew 6:33
27 Mark 10:23
28 Matthew 19:24
29 Matthew 6:24
30 Luke 9:62

4

Jesus Clashes with False Religion

From the very beginning of his public ministry Jesus clashed repeatedly with the Jewish leaders. Many of the clashes undoubtedly came from jealousy. Enormous crowds of people began to follow Jesus, and the Pharisees and the Sadducees did not like to see their power over the people so undermined. Furthermore, in their eyes, Jesus had none of the right qualifications to be a religious teacher. What could a mere carpenter from the despised area of Galilee tell anybody about God's law?

The clashes certainly did not come because Jesus attacked the Jewish religion itself. As we saw in chapter one, Jesus was born into a typical Jewish family which practised the normal Jewish observances of that time. Jesus never rejected his Jewish origins. Instead he tried to go back to the inner meaning of God's law and show people how they should apply it to their daily lives. He said that he had not come to abolish the Law or the Prophets (the writings of the Old Testament), but to fulfil them.[1]

The real problem was that the Jews at that time had surrounded the simple, basic laws of God — such as those summarized in the famous Ten Commandments — with so much extra detail that often the whole point of the Law was being missed. Jesus constantly pushed people to examine the inner core of God's commandments. And in doing this he clashed with one of the popular concepts of 'religion' itself — that the main point of religion is to keep certain rituals and observances which are supposed to please God. Jesus showed very clearly that anyone who believes in this kind of 'religion' is completely ignorant of the path of true submission to God. As we saw in the last chapter, the opening words of the 'Sermon on the Mount' pronounce the death of this kind of concept of religion.[2] Nowhere is this seen more clearly than in the various clashes that Jesus had with the Jewish authorities.

Clashes over the Sabbath

The Sabbath was (and is) the seventh day of the week which the Jews kept especially holy. This practice was based on the fourth of the 'Ten Commandments', which said that no work should be done on the Sabbath.[3] The principle of one day's rest in seven is biologically a very sound one, and it is embodied in the religious or secular laws of many countries. But the Jews of Jesus' time had made this law absurd by adding all kinds of extra prohibitions against various Sabbath activities, and so had missed the original point of the law altogether.

Jesus deliberately healed people on the Sabbath to demonstrate that God was more interested in compassion and the healing of sick bodies than in the details of religious regulations. On one Sabbath he stood up in a Jewish place of worship, the synagogue, together with a man who had a shrivelled hand. Jesus challenged the congregation: 'Which is lawful on the Sabbath: to do good or to do evil, to save life or to kill?'[4]

No one wanted to reply, and we read that Jesus was 'deeply distressed at their stubborn hearts'. So he immediately healed the man in front of them all. It was right after this incident that the Pharisees went out and started to plot how they could kill Jesus.[5]

Another dramatic healing which took place on a Sabbath was the one we considered in the last chapter, when Jesus healed the paralyzed man at the pool of Bethesda.[6] One might have thought that the Jewish leaders would be happy that a man who had been paralyzed for thirty-eight years had suddenly been healed. But instead the incident only led to further threats on Jesus' life.[7]

On one Sabbath Jesus met a man who had been blind since birth.[8] His disciples voiced the popular opinion that his blindness must be due to his sin or that of his parents. But Jesus made it perfectly clear that he was not blind as a result of sin. Instead his blindness gave an opportunity for the 'work of God' to be shown in him.[9] It almost seems as if Jesus chose the phrase '*work* of God' deliberately, knowing very well that it was the Sabbath.

Of course God still had love and compassion for people on the Sabbath! He was not restricted by petty human rules. So Jesus healed the man, who was later on brought before the Pharisees.

Their response illustrates perfectly what happens to people whose lives become dominated by religious rules. Some of the Pharisees said of Jesus, 'This man is not from God, for he does not keep the Sabbath.'

What kind of God did they believe in, if he did not even allow blind people to have their eyes opened on the Sabbath! It is clear that the attempt by the Pharisees to define minutely the 'keeping of the Sabbath' had led them into a complete distortion of God's character. But this always happens when people try to set up merely human religious regulations which do not come from God. The more we rely on man-made religion, the less we will understand the true religion which comes from God.

Before we laugh at the Pharisees for their stupidity, perhaps it is worth asking ourselves whether *we* are carrying out religious practices which do not really reflect God's love and compassion for people. We may feel very good doing these things. But the key question remains — are these practices really pleasing to God?

Clashes over prayer

The religious Jews prayed in public, and it is clear that in many cases this was so that people could see how religious they were.[10] But Jesus said that personal prayer should be in private. We should 'go into our room, close the door and pray to our Father, who is unseen'.[11] Jesus taught that if we pray in public simply so that people can see how religious we are, then the only reward is precisely that — the admiration of others. God is not interested in such praying and does not listen to it.

Jesus also said that we should not practise too much repetition while praying.[12] The religious Jews had many set prayers which they would simply 'gabble' at high speed as if the very act of saying such 'prayers' brought some benefit. But Jesus said that God does not hear us because of our many words. Instead he taught a model prayer, which is sometimes called the Lord's Prayer.[13] Jesus was not saying that this was the only prayer which the disciples should pray, but rather giving them an idea of what true prayer from the heart should be like.

If you read the prayer, you will find that it contains worship, followed by a request that God's reign should come, then a request for daily bread, then for forgiveness, and finally a plea that we might be kept from sin. It is a short prayer — simple and straight to the point. The character of true prayer is like this — that it should come from our hearts like an arrow to God.

There was something else about Jesus' teaching on prayer which did not fit the ideas of religious Jews. Jesus did not teach that we should have any special posture while praying. The Jews had all kinds of special movements of the body which were supposed to be part of prayer. But Jesus left all this on one side. God is more interested in the motives of our hearts as we pray than he is in the movements of our bodies.

Clashes over fasting

The clashes which Jesus had with Jewish practices over issues such as fasting and prayer were not like the major public confrontations which took place over the Sabbath. But the clashes were just as real, because in his insistence on the unseen relationship between the true believer and God, Jesus revealed in a devastating way the emptiness of so much religious ritual.

Fasting is another good example. It seems that in the time of Jesus many religious people only fasted so that others could see how 'holy' they were. They would even make their faces look tired and haggard to show others how much they were suffering. But Jesus said that when people wanted to fast, they should keep themselves neat and clean so that no one else would know they were fasting.[14] Fasting, like personal prayer, was something private, and should be carried out solely between the individual believer and God.

Sometimes Jesus was criticized because his disciples did not fast. But he replied that fasting was for appropriate occasions, not something to be done for its own sake alone. Fasting was for times of special need or crisis, as in his own confrontation with Satan in the desert, when he fasted for forty days. When Jesus had departed from his disciples, *then* they would have real need for fasting, during those difficult days which were to come . . .[15]

It is interesting to note how much emphasis Jesus placed on

motivation in his teachings. Two people could do exactly the same thing, such as praying or fasting, but one person would be really pleasing to God, and the other person would be far from God. What they were doing was identical, but their motives were different. One was doing it for the glory of God, the other was doing it in order to be recognized by other people.

Clashes over cleanliness

Cleanliness might seem a curious issue about which to have a clash. But the confrontation arose because some of the Pharisees spotted the disciples of Jesus eating without first having gone through the special ceremonial washing.[16] Of course everybody would wash before eating. That was not the issue. The issue was that Jesus was not following the special washing rules established in the Jewish traditions.

So the Pharisees and teachers of the Law asked Jesus, 'Why don't your disciples live according to the tradition of the elders instead of eating their food with "unclean" hands?'

Jesus replied using some words from the Old Testament: 'These people honour me with their lips, but their hearts are far from me.'[17]

That was actually the point of the issue! What did God care about ceremonial washings when people's hearts remained far from him?

Jesus continued: 'Nothing outside a man can make him "unclean" by going into him. Rather, it is what comes out of the man that makes him "unclean" . . . For out of men's hearts come evil thoughts, sexual immorality, theft, murder, adultery, greed, malice, deceit, lewdness, envy, slander, arrogance and folly. All these evils come from inside and make a man "unclean".'[18]

Cleansing the outside is very easy, but what about the inside? What about all those things Jesus bluntly lists which cause so much tragedy and grief in our own lives and in the world around us? It is not enough simply to change the environment or go through some outward cleansing ceremonies. What is really needed, said Jesus, is a radical inner cleansing . . .

Clashes over the temple

The clashes we have considered so far were all verbal debates. Jesus was certainly not afraid to criticize religious hypocrisy wherever he found it. But one clash involved force, and the reason for it is very significant. Jesus was in Jerusalem[19] just before the Passover, one of the main Jewish festivals.[20] It was a time when Jerusalem was filled with visitors from all over the Middle East. In other places we read of the many different nationalities who would be present in the city on such an occasion.[21] In the courts around the temple, Jesus found all kinds of trade going on, and the area crowded with cattle, sheep and the tables of sellers and money-changers. The Jews were using the opportunity given by crowds of visitors coming for the festival to make lots of money.

Jesus had a passionate belief in the one true God. He hated to see any disrespect for God's holiness or the places in which he was worshipped. So making a whip out of ropes, Jesus charged through the temple area, overturning the tables of the money-changers and the tradesmen, and driving the people and the cattle alike out of the area. It must have been a scene of utter confusion, with the terrified animals running in all directions and the money-changers scrabbling in the dust for their coins.

But this was no burst of merely human anger. Jesus wanted to drive home certain crucial lessons to the onlookers. 'Is it not written,' he said: ' "My house will be called a house of prayer for all nations"? But you have made it a den of robbers.'[22]

In these two quotations from the Old Testament, Jesus was making two points. First, no one who really honoured God's name could possibly allow such desecration of a holy place, especially considering the many crooked deals that were no doubt taking place within an area set aside for worshipping a holy and just God.

Second, God's temple was a house of prayer for *all* nations. What kind of message were these Jewish traders giving to the visitors present from all over the Middle East? How could they use the temple for prayer and worship when the local people seemed intent only on using it as a place for making money? God was not a God of a certain ethnic group. He was the God of the whole earth, and the God for all people and all nations. Anything that deflected from that basic vision made Jesus very angry indeed.

Something else comes out of the story which is important for us to understand. Jesus was no weakling. He must have been tough to endure forty days of fasting in the burning desert. And he must have been tough to storm the temple area and drive out the tradesmen without himself being killed on the spot by the irate mob.

Clashes with religious hypocrisy

In a sense most of the clashes we have looked at so far have been connected with religious hypocrisy. There was one particular occasion though when Jesus clashed very directly with the 'teachers of the Law and the Pharisees' on this issue. He was addressing his disciples and the crowds in general at the time. But it is very obvious that the Pharisees were present, perhaps listening at the back of the crowd, because often in his speech Jesus addressed them directly.

The speech, recorded in Matthew 23, makes the rhetoric of some of today's religious leaders look quite mild in comparison. In fact none of us can escape Jesus' devastating analysis of our own hypocrisy. His words have as much relevance for today as when they were first spoken nearly 2,000 years ago.

Jesus hit out at those religious leaders who expect other people to do all kinds of religious observances, but then are not willing to practise what they preach themselves.[23]

Then he scorned religious leaders who were full of pomp and had a great sense of their own importance. They even wore special clothes such as prayer shawls with extra-long tassels to show everyone how much they prayed.[24] These were the type of people who liked the place of honour at banquets and wanted everyone to show them respect and call them by special names in public. But Jesus said very bluntly that such people had no place in the kingdom of heaven and instead deserved hell.[25] He condemned the practice of using special names for religious leaders. He said that only God deserves to be called Master. 'For whoever exalts himself will be humbled, and whoever humbles himself will be exalted.'[26]

But you may know of many Christian churches where people wear special religious clothes and sit in special places, and even have special names! This only shows how very far some who claim to follow Jesus have departed from what he actually taught. Remember though that the motives are the key. If a religious leader has a special name in order to distinguish his particular function or job, there is nothing wrong with that if his job involves serving other people. But if he uses the name to try to be the 'big boss', then that person is far from the clear teachings of Jesus.

When it came to the subject of swearing, Jesus called the religious leaders 'blind fools!'[27] They were teaching that oaths could be valid or non-valid according to the object by which they were being sworn. But here, and elsewhere, Jesus taught that those who follow God do not need to swear at all.[28] 'Simply let your "yes" be "yes",' said Jesus, 'and your "no" be "no"; anything beyond this comes from the evil one.' Our speech should be the simple truth. If we swear by something else, then it implies that without the oath we may be telling lies. But this level of honesty is far below that demanded by the kingdom of God.

'Giving' was another topic on which Jesus had some hard words for all hypocrites.[29] The Pharisees were very concerned about giving to God exactly one-tenth of all their crops — even down to tiny quantities of herbs such as mint. But Jesus called them blind guides! They were so taken up by these stupid details, that they were neglecting the really important issues in God's law, such as 'justice, mercy and faithfulness'. Jesus said that they were like people removing dirt from milk who 'strain out a gnat but swallow a camel!'

The speech of Jesus recorded in Matthew 23 comes to an incredible climax when he calls the Pharisees 'snakes' and a 'brood of vipers'. Their central problem was that they were putting on a nice clean exterior, but inside they were 'full of greed and self-indulgence'.[30] They were like white tombs, which look beautiful on the outside, but inside are full of dead men's bones.[31] Despite their pleasant-sounding words, they were in fact the kind of people who murdered the prophets that God sent.[32]

Again, Jesus' words have astonishing relevance for our own day. How often apparently nice religious leaders, who look so good on TV or when interviewed in the newspapers, behave in a way exactly the opposite to what they say! How much hatred there is which goes under the guise of religious respectability. How much jealousy is covered by nice-looking religious garments. How much lust goes on in the hearts of those who can cover the darkness of their lives with beautiful-sounding religious words, but who cannot hide the blackness of their own hearts from God.

Jesus was never afraid to speak out clearly and to confront the hypocrisy of all our hearts. The kingdom of God is like a brilliant light which shows up the dust and dirt in our lives. No one can escape its blinding glare.

There is one area of clash that we have not yet touched on. This, in fact, is the most important one of all. It is Jesus' clash with the Jews concerning his astonishing claims about himself. These claims ultimately led to his death. But first we need to look more closely at how Jesus analyzed the needs of the world around him.

1   Matthew 5:17
2   Matthew 5:3
3   Exodus 20:8–11
4   Mark 3:4
5   Mark 3:6
6   John 5:1–15
7   John 5:16–18
8   John 9:1–41
9   John 9:3
10 Matthew 6:5
11 Matthew 6:6
12 Matthew 6:7
13 Matthew 6:9–13
14 Matthew 6:16–18
15 Luke 5:33–39
16 Mark 7:1–4
17 Mark 7:5–8
18 Mark 7:15, 21–23

19 Mark 11:15–17
20 John 2:13–17
21 Acts 2:5–11
22 Mark 11:17
23 Matthew 23:2–4
24 Matthew 23:5–7
25 Matthew 23:13–15
26 Matthew 23:12
27 Matthew 23:18–22
28 Matthew 5:33–37
29 Matthew 23:23–24
30 Matthew 23:25–26
31 Matthew 23:27
32 Matthew 23:31–36

5
Jesus and Social Justice

One of the problems about examining the teachings of Jesus Christ is that most people connect him so closely with 'Christianity'! But unfortunately there are many things today which receive the label 'Christianity' even though they have little to do with Jesus Christ. In fact sometimes these so-called 'Christian' things are opposite to what Jesus taught!

This problem becomes particularly acute when we start thinking about 'Christian' attitudes to politics, social justice and so on. Many people think that there are such things as 'Christian' countries, and therefore that the international policies of such countries must in some way reflect the teachings of Jesus Christ.

As we have already seen from the teachings of Jesus on the kingdom of God, such a concept is quite impossible. There is not and cannot be such a thing as a 'Christian' country. The 'boundaries' of the kingdom of God bear no resemblance to any geographical or political boundaries. God's reign is for all people everywhere who will submit themselves to him. He is not the God of any particular country or ethnic group.

It may be that some countries have adopted Christianity as their official or state religion. It may be that in certain countries Christianity happens to be the majority religion. It may even be that a political leader in some country will proclaim his support of some Christian teaching. But none of these things make a country a 'Christian' country.

So no one can look at the political record of a so-called 'Christian' country and say 'Ah, this is a "Christian" country, so what it is doing represents the priorities of the kingdom of God.' In fact, the true followers of Jesus may be a minority even in those countries which are looked upon as being 'Christian'. The actual numbers of such followers of Jesus may be far greater in a country which is officially known as being 'atheist' or where there is a different state religion.

Another idea which can distort our thinking is the concept that in some sense Christianity is a 'Western' religion. It is true that Europe was one of the main areas where Christianity was believed and taught for many centuries. But the culture and context of Jesus and his teachings is Middle Eastern. And there are far more true followers of Jesus today in continents such as Africa and South America than there are in Europe.

The teachings of Jesus were given for all people at all places and at all times. This is especially important to remember when we come to look at what he said about social justice, because we need to consider carefully what he actually said, not what some nominal Christians may have done in his name in later centuries.

Did Jesus have a political programme?

Some people try to interpret the life of Jesus in purely political terms. However, as we have already seen, Jesus refused all the attempts which were made to turn him merely into a local political leader who would challenge the authority of the emperor in Rome, but whose power would only be worldly power.[1] Nor did Jesus lay down any specific political programme which would lead by direct steps to the overthrow of Roman imperialism or to the changing of the political *status quo* in first-century Palestine.

Was Jesus, then, one who withdrew from the world? One who saw his mission only in terms of intangible 'spiritual' issues? Certainly not, as we have already begun to see.

The life of Jesus was set right in the middle of human need and suffering. He lived with the people in the midst of their need, not set apart in some isolated place where he would remain untouched by the reality of pain and injustice.

His teaching and mission on earth were far more radical than a limited political programme which would have relevance only for a certain economic structure and moment in history. In fact the impact of Jesus' life was destined to be felt in social reforms in immensely different eras and political systems. This is because the kingdom of God deals with the heart of man and the very roots of his dilemmas, not just with adjustments in his environment.

The teaching of Jesus on social justice was intensely subversive of all opposition to the kingdom of God. If we again take the picture of a shapeless piece of dough, the teaching was not given to beat the dough into a certain fixed shape, but rather like the yeast to change its whole character from within, so that its very nature would be transformed.

Jesus did not just teach about social justice — he actually lived it in his daily relationship with people. And both in his life and in his teaching he focused on five crucial points which are fundamental if there is to be any true justice in society.

The absolute worth of the individual

Jesus was born and brought up in a tightly-knit small-town community. Probably most people in the area were related to each other. As a carpenter-builder, Jesus had been a familiar figure in the area for many years, travelling around to serve the practical needs of the people.

When Jesus started his public ministry, it is therefore especially striking that he placed such emphasis on the worth of the individual. It is very easy for one person's needs to become swallowed up in the crowd, especially if that person is weak, or sick, or despised for some reason by others.

Jesus constantly underlines the fact that the kingdom of God is for the poor and the oppressed, for those whom society tends to ignore, for those who are unable to help themselves. Although he was so often surrounded by crowds of people pressing in on him, Jesus was always quick to pick out the needy individual.

One day Jesus was on his way to heal the dying twelve-year-old daughter of the ruler of the synagogue.[2] Since the man had an important position in local society, one might have expected that Jesus would hurry to heal the daughter before it was too late, but the crowds almost crushed him as he went. Buried in the crowd was a woman who had been subject to bleeding for twelve years. Not wanting to bother Jesus, who was obviously on an important mission, she came up behind him and simply touched the edge of his cloak.

'Who touched me?' Jesus asked.

The disciples protested, 'Master, the people are crowding and pressing against you.'

But Jesus said, 'Someone touched me; I know that power has gone out from me.'

The woman, realizing that she had been discovered, fell trembling at the feet of Jesus and told him what she had done.

Jesus said to her, 'Daughter, your faith has healed you. Go in peace.'

One needy woman in the middle of a crowd! But Jesus had time for her, and the important man in local society had to wait while Jesus cared for her particular need.

The fact that Jesus cared for the needs of women at all seemed extraordinary in a society in which power and prestige lay very much in the hands of men. The Jews had carefully adjusted religious laws to make sure that women remained second-class citizens. Jesus revolutionized attitudes to women by his own attitudes and by treating them as equals.

One day Jesus was returning to his home area of Galilee through Samaria.[3] Samaria was where the Samaritans lived — Jews who had intermarried with the surrounding races over the years, and so who were despised by the other Jews for not being racially and religiously pure. Many Jews would even avoid travelling through Samaria if they could help it to avoid being contaminated by such people. Jesus had no time for such racialism.

Since it was very hot and Jesus was tired, he sat down on Jacob's well at a little town called Sychar. It was midday and he was alone because his disciples had gone into the town to buy food. At that moment a Samaritan woman came up. Of course, nobody would normally come to draw water under the heat of the midday sun, so it was obvious that the woman wanted to avoid the other women of the town. Jesus asked her for a drink of water. The woman was amazed that he, a Jew, would ask her, a Samaritan — and a woman at that — for a drink.[4]

Soon Jesus was engaged in conversation with her, and it quickly became clear why she was a social outcast.[5] But Jesus spent just as much time and care in counselling this one woman, who was rejected even by her own community, as he had with a member of the Jewish Council just a short while before.[6] Both were equal in God's sight.

On another occasion Jesus was teaching in one of the Jewish synagogues, when he noticed in the congregation a hunchbacked woman bent over double.[7] He healed her immediately, but the synagogue ruler was indignant because Jesus had once again healed on the Sabbath. Jesus answered him, 'You hypocrites! Doesn't each of you on the Sabbath untie his ox or donkey from the stall and lead it out to give it water? Then should not this woman, a daughter of Abraham, whom Satan has kept bound for eighteen long years, be set free on the Sabbath day from what bound her?'[8]

The Jews were very proud of being 'sons of Abraham', but it was always the *men* who emphasized that they were *sons* of Abraham! Jesus deliberately stresses the point that *daughters* of Abraham are just as important as the sons! And what religious Jew would not let his animals out to have a drink on the Sabbath? So were they really claiming that feeding a donkey was of more importance than healing a sick woman? In fact this is precisely what they were claiming, so it is not surprising that we read, 'all Jesus' opponents were humiliated by his words'.[9]

Children were another class of people who could easily be excluded from the busy life of a religious leader. But Jesus always had time for them. On one occasion people were bringing little children to Jesus so that he could touch them and bless them.[10] The disciples tried to stop them. Don't disturb Jesus! He's tired and too busy!

But when Jesus saw what was going on, he was indignant and said to them, 'Let the little children come to me . . . for the kingdom of God belongs to such as these.'

Then Jesus continued with some quite extraordinary words, 'I tell you the truth, anyone who will not receive the kingdom of God like a little child will never enter it.'

What could Jesus mean?

Later on he had some incredibly blunt words of warning for anyone preventing children from entering the kingdom of God.[11] With a small child standing there in the middle of them, Jesus said, 'If anyone causes one of these little ones who believe in me to sin, it would be better for him to have a large millstone hung around his neck and be drowned in the depths of the sea.'

Jesus was always the defender of the weak and of those who had no one to fight for their rights in society. He resisted the proud and the rich at every opportunity and poured scorn on pompous religious people. But his heart was open to the oppressed. When he was criticized for eating with the despised people in society, Jesus replied that 'it is not the healthy who need a doctor, but the sick.'[12]

Once when Jesus was eating in the house of a prominent Pharisee, he told his host, 'When you give a banquet, invite the poor, the cripple, the lame, the blind, and you will be blessed.'[13]

Jesus summarized his ministry by quoting from some prophetic words in the Old Testament book of Isaiah which had been written some 800 years before his birth. He read these words in the synagogue in his own home town of Nazareth:

> The Spirit of the Lord is on me,
> because he has anointed me
> to preach good news to the poor.
> He has sent me to proclaim freedom for the prisoners
> and recovery of sight for the blind,
> to release the oppressed,
> to proclaim the year of the Lord's favour.[14]

Then Jesus said to the congregation, 'Today this Scripture is fulfilled in your hearing.'

Every individual has absolute worth in the sight of God. There can be no social justice without that basic starting point. As long as one segment of society is crushing another either by force or by neglect, then there can be no real justice. And once people become pawns or stepping-stones towards some 'higher purpose' for society, which means that they themselves are trodden down in the process, then there can be no social justice. People can never be like eggs which have to be broken in order to make a nice omelette. It is the people themselves who are of value right now, not the theoretical society of the future which everyone dreams of, but which somehow never seems to come.

Of course social justice does not develop automatically in a society simply because a few people start believing that each individual in that society has absolute value. But it is a crucial starting point for the struggle for reform, for the passing of new laws, for the fight to defend the right of the poor, and for resistance against the oppressor.

And Jesus said that those who accept the kingdom of God are like salt in society.[15] You need only a little 'salt' to affect radically the way in which society functions. The belief in the basic worth of the individual is the 'glue' which keeps society together. If you have lived in a country where there is some basic respect for the rights of the individual, you will certainly understand what Jesus is talking about at this point.

Like most teachings which contain a great truth, the exaggeration of that truth produces error. In some places the belief in the worth of the individual has been exaggerated into individualism, where each person creates his own private world. In such societies the 'self' and the health, advancement and projection of the 'self' on others becomes all-important.

The kingdom of God runs directly against such individualism. People in the kingdom are not like islands on a sea of selfishness. They are more like the parts of a body. Each part has value in itself, but is nevertheless working for the good of the whole. When one part ceases to function properly, then the whole community suffers.

The blasphemy of racialism

The roots of racialism lie in the belief that people do not have absolute worth — they only have relative worth. Because one group of people have a different language, culture, historical background and perhaps skin colour, they are looked down upon by another group of people. That is blasphemy. It is blasphemy because it is implicitly stating something false about God, the Creator. It is suggesting that the great Creator God made people with relative worth according to their genes and environment. Anyone believing that has no place in God's kingdom.

Jesus undermined every form of racialism both in emphasizing the worth of the individual, as we have already seen, and also by deliberately showing that the kingdom of God was equally for all men and women whatever their racial background might be.

It is certainly true that the public ministry of Jesus was mainly among the Jews. These were, after all, his people. It was the Jews that he was mainly meeting in his daily work of healing and teaching. But within a few years of the end of Jesus' ministry on earth, the teaching of the kingdom of God had exploded out of the Jewish world and into the dozens of races and ethnic groups which made up the Roman Empire. The seeds of that explosion were embedded firmly in the acts and teaching of Jesus himself.

The Jews at the time of Jesus generally interpreted their religion in a racialist way. They felt that their beliefs made them superior to non-Jews. They looked down on other ethnic groups living around them, and conveniently forgot the many places in the Old Testament where God reminded the Jews that he was not showing kindness to them because they were a significant race, but because they were so small and *in*significant.

There was nothing that infuriated the Jews more than being reminded by Jesus that God cared just as much about other races as he did for them. The Jews in Jesus' home town of Nazareth were no exception. When Jesus was reading the Old Testament in the synagogue at Nazareth, he quoted the words from the prophet Isaiah about the poor and the oppressed that we have already mentioned.[16] After Jesus had said, 'Today this Scripture is fulfilled in your hearing', we read that 'all spoke well of him and were amazed at the gracious words that came from his lips'.[17]

A preacher who just wanted to please his hearers would have finished right there. But Jesus quickly realized that these people in his own home town who knew him so well, had not really understood what he was trying to say. So he continued, 'I tell you the truth, no prophet is accepted in his home town.'

Then Jesus went on to give examples from the Old Testament of two famous prophets that God had sent to *non*-Jews in order to show his power.[18] One was Elijah the prophet, whom God had sent to help a poor widow in the non-Jewish area of Sidon with her supply of food during a time of famine. The other was Elisha, the prophet God had sent to heal Naaman, the captain of the Syrian army who had leprosy. Just to drive the point right home, Jesus remarked, 'And there were many in Israel with leprosy in the time of Elisha the prophet, yet not one of them was cleansed — only Naaman the Syrian.'

So God loved the Lebanese and the Syrians and cared for them just as much as he did for the Jews! It was hardly surprising that we read 'all the people in the synagogue were furious when they heard this' and drove Jesus right out of the town! They even tried to kill Jesus, but he escaped. Such is the fate of those who speak out against racialism.

In his famous parable called the 'Good Samaritan', Jesus later showed that it is not enough to be against racialism. We actually have to be involved ourselves in meeting the needs of others who come from a different background from our own.

It all started when an expert in Jewish law stood up to test Jesus.[19]

'Teacher,' he asked, 'what must I do to inherit eternal life?'

So Jesus challenged him to quote what was written in the Old Testament law.

The man answered very correctly, ' "Love the Lord your God with all your heart and with all your soul and with all your strength and with all your mind"; and "Love your neighbour as yourself." '

That sounded very good. What a nice place the world would be if everyone would only love their neighbour as much as they love themselves!

But at this point the legal expert made a tactical error.

'And who is my neighbour?' he asked Jesus.

Perhaps later he regretted ever asking the question, because Jesus then went on to tell the devastating story of the Good Samaritan.

A man was travelling on the road from Jerusalem to Jericho when he was attacked by robbers, beaten up and left half-dead by the side of the road. A Jewish priest happened to be going the same way, but when he saw the man lying by the roadside, he carefully walked by on the other side. What might happen if he stopped? Why, he might have to get involved with the man's needs — *his* religious business was so urgent . . . Then a Levite came along. The Levites were one of the twelve tribes of Israel, the tribe which had been appointed to perform priestly duties in Israel. So they felt themselves to be 'especially chosen' even within the Jewish community itself, and tended to look down on all the other tribes. But, said Jesus, this Levite fellow did exactly the same as the ordinary priest — he too passed by on the other side of the road!

Then along came a Samaritan. As we saw earlier, the Samaritans as a race were totally despised by the Jews, because they were originally pure Jews who had then intermarried with people from the surrounding nations. So Jesus deliberately chose a Samaritan for the story because of the racial implications.

And what did the Samaritan do? He saw the half-dead man and had pity on him. He stopped to bandage and dress his wounds. Then he put the man on his own donkey, brought him to an inn and took care of him the whole night. The following day he left some of his own money with the innkeeper for the wounded man and promised to pay him more later if there were any extra expenses!

Jesus said to the legal expert, 'Which of these three do you think was a neighbour to the man who fell into the hands of robbers?'

The man replied, 'The one who had mercy on him.'

Jesus told him, 'Go and do likewise.'

It is very easy to believe that someone is our 'neighbour' when they come from the same background as we do, and especially when there is a possibility that they will pay us back later when *we* have a need. But Jesus showed that real love does not expect anything in return. In fact so different is this kind of love from anything we find elsewhere, that the New Testament writers had to find a new Greek word to express the concept. It was the word *agape*. *Agape* is the love that expects nothing in return. It is a fundamental weapon in the fight against racialism.

It seems incredible that in some so-called 'Christian' countries there should be laws asserting the superiority of one race over another. Even the simplest, most basic teaching of Jesus is totally opposed to such laws!

But, let us face it, we all tend to be hypocrites when it comes to the subject of racialism. It is very easy to thunder away in a self-righteous tone of voice about the terrible racialism in some other country. But what about the despised communities in our own countries? What are we doing to help them? Race is not just about colour, but also about ethnic groups who have little voice in the nation's affairs. We should not be so taken up with the failings of others that we forget the racialism that may be on our own doorsteps. We may have become so used to it that we can hardly recognize it for what it really is . . .

The curse of riches

If you had to guess what Jesus taught about riches simply by observing the behaviour of some large Christian churches and institutions today, then you might be forgiven for thinking that Jesus taught the value of accumulating wealth. In fact he taught precisely the opposite.

Not only did Jesus teach the opposite, but he reserved some of his strongest condemnations for those whose main aim in life was to accumulate personal wealth. He once told a story about a farmer who had an excellent harvest.[20] There was so much produce that the farmer had no room to store it. So he pulled down his small barns and built bigger ones. Finally the work was complete and his big barns were packed with produce.

He said to himself, 'You have plenty of good things laid up for many years. Take life easy; eat, drink and be merry.'

'But', continued Jesus, 'God said to him, "You fool! This very night your life will be demanded from you. Then who will get what you have prepared for yourself?"'

Jesus summarized the main point of the story: 'This is how it will be with anyone who stores up things for himself but is not rich towards God.'

Once we have been freed from the craving for riches, continued Jesus, then the basis for so much human worry simply disappears.[21] How the pressures of materialistic societies cause people to worry and fret! What will the neighbours think if we don't have the latest car? And how much fretting and anxiety comes over whether people have the latest fashions!

But Jesus said, 'Do not set your heart on what you will eat or drink; do not worry about it. For the pagan world runs after all such things, and your Father knows that you need them. But seek his kingdom and these things will be given to you as well.'

'Sell your possessions and give to the poor', commanded Jesus, 'for where your treasure is, there your heart will be also.'[22]

What a revolution would occur if people started obeying the simple teaching of Jesus! Like so much of what he said, it goes far deeper than merely suggesting changes in political structures, however important they may be. His teaching in fact undermines what much of the world's wars and struggles are all about, both on an individual scale and on a national scale. As one of Jesus' followers later expressed it: 'The love of money is the root of all kinds of evil.'[23]

How many struggles there are between communities to obtain financial power! And how many wars are fought over insignificant pieces of land, with hundreds of thousands of people being killed and wounded in the process, just so that one nation's area might be increased by a few per cent! And on an individual level how many blood feuds, murders, fights and arguments are generated every day of the week simply by love of money!

The priorities of the kingdom of God mean that we 'cannot serve both God and money'.[24] God must come first. It is not that the money, wealth and possessions are wrong in themselves. There is no hint in the teachings of Jesus of the Greek philosophy that maintains that immaterial, 'spiritual' things are in some way 'higher' than earthly, physical things. No, riches can become a curse, said Jesus, because they can so easily grip our hearts and lead to self-complacency or to a selfish greed for more. When the kingdom of God comes first, then the other things in our lives will begin to assume their right proportion.

This teaching cuts right across debates about the 'rich' and the 'poor'. It gives a totally new perspective. Neither being rich nor being poor is of any advantage in the kingdom of God. What counts is whether our hearts have become detached from the craving for accumulating power and wealth for ourselves. The same craving may be in the heart of the poor as it is in the heart of the rich. Some of the most materialistic people are those who were recently poor and now have become rich. Whether you are poor or whether you are rich, if money is your master, then you have no place in the kingdom of God.

There was a rich young ruler in the time of Jesus who had to learn this lesson the hard way. One day he asked Jesus, 'Good teacher, what must I do to inherit eternal life?'[25]

Jesus gave a puzzling reply, which we will turn to in a later chapter: 'Why do you call me good? No one is good — except God alone. You know the commandments: "Do not commit adultery, do not murder, do not steal, do not give false testimony, honour your father and mother."'

Notice that Jesus deliberately omitted the very first of the Ten Commandments in which God says 'You shall have no other gods before me.'[26] Instead he quoted to the man the commandments which relate more to social relationships. And we can almost picture the man ticking off each commandment in his mind as he listened to Jesus.

'All these I have kept since I was a boy.'

When Jesus heard this he said to him, 'You still lack one thing. Sell everything you have and give to the poor, and you will have treasure in heaven. Then come, follow me.'

Then we read that the man became very sad, because he was a man of great wealth.

Jesus looked at him and said, 'How hard it is for the rich to enter the kingdom of God! Indeed, it is easier for a camel to go through the eye of a needle than for a rich man to enter the kingdom of God.'

Everyone listening protested, 'Who then can be saved?'

Jesus replied, 'What is impossible with man is possible with God.'

What is Jesus saying here? Is he telling the rich young ruler that if he gives up his wealth then he will receive eternal life in return as a kind of reward? No. The real problem for the ruler was not that he possessed many treasures, but rather that his treasures possessed *him*. He was disobeying the first commandment. He certainly did have 'other gods' besides God. In his case his god was his money. Other people have other 'gods'. It may be their career and their driving ambition to reach the top. It may be a wrong relationship which has become the all-consuming passion of their lives. It may even be something very legitimate and good in itself — like a wife, husband or children. But Jesus made clear that whenever something else in our lives takes on such importance that it replaces the centrality of God himself, then we have 'other gods' in our lives and we are breaking the first commandment.

That is why it takes a special miracle for a rich person to enter the kingdom of God, because it means that he has to give up one master in order to serve another. You cannot serve God and money at the same time . . .

We can see why Jesus had a special sympathy for the poor. It was not because the poor had a greater value than others, or because Jesus was biased in some way towards poor people, but rather that poor people would have a greater chance of understanding what the kingdom of God was all about. Their hearts were not so likely to be gripped by the tin gods of this world.

At the same time, the compassion of Jesus flowed towards anyone in need. He certainly was concerned about the basic physical needs of the poor. He did not tell people just to sell their possessions, but to sell their possessions and give to the poor. There had to be an actual redistribution of wealth, not just the giving up of wealth itself. The value of the individual meant that everyone had the basic human right of food, shelter and protection within society.

But it was no answer at all for rich people to be overthrown and for poor people to become rich! No, that was far too superficial. As a follower of Jesus later put it: 'If we have food and clothing, we will be content with that.'[27] Once the basic needs of life have been met, then why worry about accumulating more than that? It will lead only to pain, greed and war.

If we apply the teaching of Jesus on riches, does this mean that the gap between rich and poor will automatically dissolve away in our societies? Unfortunately not. The world is too complicated a place for that. But what the teaching does give is a basis with which to start the struggle. If you do not even believe that every individual made by God has equal worth, then you will not even think of starting such a struggle. Why bother? There has to be some motivation to even begin.

Once the driving force is there, then all kinds of things start to happen. There is pressure to change laws. Unjust landlords are brought to court. Bribery is attacked. Tax laws are not only passed to reduce the gap between rich and poor, but they are actually enforced in a just way. People start to listen to those sections of society which normally have no voice in the affairs of the nation. Pressure groups build up to push for a fairer distribution of wealth.

The yeast of the kingdom begins to do its own inner life-giving work.

The futility of violence

Jesus was born into a world in which the use of violence as a way to achieve political goals was extremely common. It seems that the world has not changed very much since then . . .

Imperial Rome, like most imperial powers, did not hesitate to use overwhelming force whenever necessary in order to crush all forms of opposition. In 4 BC the Roman General Varus is reported to have crucified 2,000 Jewish rebels against Rome. The crucifixion of 3,600 Jews by Florus in AD 66 precipitated a major Jewish rebellion. During the subsequent siege of Jerusalem by Titus in AD 70, so many were crucified that there was a shortage of wood. In enemy-occupied Palestine it must have been a common occurrence to see small processions of people carrying a *patibulum*, the crossbeam which was fixed to an upright post to form a cross, making their way out of Jerusalem to the traditional spot for crucifixion outside the city walls.

Nor were the powerful untouched by religious intrigue and violence. As we saw in chapter one, when Jesus was born, Herod the Great was the ruler of Palestine. He was an absolute tyrant who killed anyone who opposed him — including all those children less than two years old in the town of Bethlehem soon after the birth of Jesus. Even by the barbaric standards of our own day, a dictator who ordered the cold-blooded killing of hundreds of babies must have been extremely ruthless. Just how ruthless Herod was we see later on in his life when he executed Mariamne, one of his wives. He was also involved in the murder of two of his own sons, Alexander and Aristobulus, because they opposed his orders. Just five years before Herod died, he ordered the execution of yet another of his sons, Antipater, who was due to succeed him. Those who lived in first-century Palestine were certainly used to violence!

It seems all the more amazing, then, that Jesus refused to

follow the way of violence in order to achieve his goals. He had a large following among the masses. Though unpopular with the authorities, he was immensely popular with the common people during much of his public ministry. If he had ordered his followers to arm and march upon the Roman army barracks in Jerusalem, there is no doubt that thousands of them would have been ready to obey. So why did Jesus choose such a different way?

One reason, as we have already been seeing, is that the way of violence is useless when it comes to changing men's hearts. Geographical boundaries can be changed through violence. Political power can be won through violence. Economic domination can be obtained through violence. But violence is a hopeless tool for winning the allegiance of people's hearts.

This is precisely why Jesus came — to win the allegiance of people's hearts for the kingdom of God. As God's kingdom was a spiritual kingdom, not a geographical kingdom, it was pointless to fight for it. True love can never be forced love.

It was a hard lesson for his disciples to learn. They were very much people of their age. Perhaps Jesus deliberately chose Simon the Zealot as one of his followers to demonstrate how different the way of God's kingdom really was. The founder of the Zealots was a man called Judas who, like Jesus, came from Galilee, and who led a Jewish revolt against Rome in AD 6. The guerrilla movement which Judas established continued right up to the destruction of Jerusalem in AD 70, and perhaps beyond that time as well.

How many times during daily life with Jesus must Simon the Zealot have longed to grab his sword and deal with the opposition once and for all! He was not the only one of Jesus' disciples who was tempted to take this path.

Among the disciples of Jesus were two brothers called James and John. One day they were all travelling together through Samaria towards Jerusalem.[28] Messengers were sent ahead of the group into a Samaritan village in order to make arrangements for that night's hospitality. But the people of the village did not welcome Jesus because they had heard that he was travelling to Jerusalem. That was not *their* capital! Why should they give hospitality to these hated Jewish purists!

When James and John heard this, they were disgusted.

'Lord,' they asked Jesus, 'do you want us to call fire down from heaven to destroy them?'

That seemed to be the perfect solution! If you have the power, why not use it? Zap! The opposition is gone. But Jesus turned and reproved them, and they went to another village instead. He had come to save, not to destroy.

If ever there was a time when violence was called for, then it was when Jesus himself was arrested. The arrest was carried out by a large crowd armed with swords and clubs.[29] Peter, one of his disciples, who always had been a bit of a hot-head, immediately reached for his sword and made a swipe at the hostile crowd, cutting off the ear of one of the high priest's servants in the process. It was the natural, instinctive reaction of a man who wanted to defend his master.

But Jesus would have none of it.

'Put your sword back in its place,' Jesus ordered him, 'for all who draw the sword will die by the sword.'

How those words echo down the centuries! The futility of violence is that it so often causes more violence. People are always talking about 'the war to end all wars' — and then they proceed to have another one. Violence sows seeds of hatred and revenge, and its bitter harvest is reaped over generations to come. People like to talk about the final solution, but they cannot seem to learn from history that violent solutions are rarely final.

The path of violence is not the way of the kingdom of God. Of course God had the power to deliver Jesus from arrest if he so wanted to. Jesus himself said to Peter as he healed the severed ear of the high priest's servant, 'Do you think I cannot call on my father, and he will at once put at my disposal more than twelve legions of angels? But how then would the Scriptures be fulfilled that say it must happen in this way?'[30]

But Jesus was not leading a rebellion. As he asked the crowd, 'Am I leading a rebellion, that you have come out with swords and clubs to capture me?'[31]

The way of the kingdom of God was the way of peace. It was the way of capturing people's hearts and minds through love. And the only way that Jesus could generate that kind of love was by renouncing the way of violence and letting himself fall quite deliberately into the hands of violent men . . .

The reality of judgment

If you believe that the fight for social justice is restricted only to this world, then you have a problem. Because however successful the fight may be, it will never be totally successful. Certainly in our own lifetime, at least, there will always be the poor and the deprived who will never receive full justice from their own societies. With the world's prisons filling with political prisoners, whose only 'crime' is that they hold the wrong opinions, there are thousands of people wasting away their lives in confinement. Many are being tortured. What kind of justice are they going to receive? Of course we should be fighting for their rights now. The ethics of the kingdom of God demand it. But, to be realistic, do we really think we are going to put *every* injustice right in this area?

What about the monstrous dictators of this world? Those who have been responsible for the deaths of millions, but who themselves suffered little for their crimes. Was a suicide bullet enough justice for a man like Hitler?

If you believe that the present world is the only theatre for the exercise of justice, then ultimately the very concept of justice itself becomes eroded and meaningless. It is very clear that the world is a very unjust place because of human evil. Some murderers go free, while some innocent people are imprisoned for murders that they never committed. Many people slave away their lives in daily labour simply to fill their stomachs, while others do nothing themselves but profit from others' labours. True, we can fight against that kind of injustice right now — but do you expect total justice in your lifetime? What about justice for all the people who are going to live *before* the dawning of your 'golden age' when everything will be put right?

There is only one way which ensures a solid foundation for justice in the present life, and that is the assurance that there will be an ultimate justice in the next. Jesus taught clearly the reality of such justice. It was a justice based on the fact of God's future judgment on all people of all races, at whatever time of history they lived, in such a way that *all* their words, *all* their acts, *all* the

ways in which they had oppressed others, would finally be
brought to the bar of God's ultimate justice.

The word 'judgment' has the meaning of 'condemnation' for
many people. But that is not the only meaning of the word as
used by Jesus. On his lips it becomes a word, yes, of warning, but
also of tremendous encouragement, because it means that the
very limited form of justice we are seeing in the present life is not
the end of the story.

Those who were religious hypocrites, said Jesus, would have to
face the reality of God's judgment. To those who were murderers
under the guise of religion, he cried, 'You snakes! You brood of
vipers! How will you escape being condemned to hell?'[32]

In fact those who devalued other people by anger or by calling
them fools, let alone actually committing physical murder,
would, Jesus said, be 'in danger of the fire of hell'.[33] And the
person who devalued the body of a woman who was not his wife
by lusting after her had already committed adultery in his heart
and was in danger of hell.[34] Far better to be a cripple for life than
to be the cause of other people falling away from the realities of
God's kingdom and so be 'thrown into eternal fire'.[35]

Hell, for Jesus, was not some mythical entity which he used as
a kind of stick with which to beat people into moral submission.
Rather, it was the reality of eternal separation from God's
kingdom.

Jesus taught that the decisions we make in this life are irreversible. How we spend our lives has eternal consequences. There is
no crossing from one side to the other once we die. If we choose
for God's kingdom in this life, then that choice is an eternal
choice. If we choose against his kingdom, then *that* choice is for
ever as well.

'A time is coming', said Jesus, 'when all who are in their graves
will hear God's voice and come out — those who have done good
will arise to live, and those who have done evil will rise to be
condemned.'[36]

When we live with the perspective of eternal justice, then even
the common events of everyday life are given a new significance.
Once Jesus pictured to his disciples what it would be like on the
great judgment day, when finally we will have to give account for
all our deeds.[37] He pictured himself as the King, sitting on his

throne, separating the 'sheep and the goats' — those who did the works of the kingdom of God and those who rejected them.

To those on one side the King said, 'Come . . . take your inheritance, the kingdom prepared for you since the creation of the world. For I was hungry and you gave me something to eat, I was thirsty and you gave me something to drink, I was a stranger and you invited me in, I needed clothes and you clothed me, I was sick and you looked after me, I was in prison and you came to visit me.'

Then his listeners began to protest, 'But Lord, when did we do these things to *you*?'

And, in the story of Jesus, the King replies, 'Whatever you did for one of the least of these brothers of mine, you did for me.'

Then the King turns to the group on the other side and says, 'Depart from me, you who are cursed, into the eternal fire prepared for the devil and his angels.'

These are the people who never demonstrated in this life the works of the kingdom of God. They never fed the hungry, or gave hospitality to strangers, or clothed the poor, or visited the sick or those in prison.[38]

'Then they will go away to eternal punishment,' said Jesus, 'but the righteous to eternal life.'

So in this life nothing is random. Nothing is meaningless. Justice has eternal significance. Life is not a play in the theatre of the absurd which ends with the actors throwing away their masks. We are not dice being rolled around by our genes and by our environment. Justice matters. Poverty matters. Racialism matters. All our deeds which reflect our concern — or lack of concern — for the absolute worth of the individual have consequences which will never end.

That is the awesome responsibility of being a human being made by God.

1   John 6:15
2   Luke 8:40–48
3   John 4:4–42
4   John 4:9
5   John 4:18
6   John 3:1–21

7   Luke 13:10–13
8   Luke 13:14–16
9   Luke 13:17
10 Mark 10:13–16
11 Matthew 18:6
12 Matthew 9:10–13
13 Luke 14:13
14 Luke 4:16–21
15 Matthew 5:13
16 Luke 4:16–21
17 Luke 4:22
18 Luke 4:24–27
19 Luke 10:25–37
20 Luke 12:13–21
21 Luke 12:22–34
22 Luke 12:32, 34
23 1 Timothy 6:10
24 Luke 16:13
25 Luke 18:18–27
26 Exodus 20:3
27 1 Timothy 6:8
28 Luke 9:51–56
29 Matthew 26:47–56
30 Matthew 26:53–54
31 Matthew 26:55
32 Matthew 23:33
33 Matthew 5:21–22
34 Matthew 5:27–30
35 Matthew 18:6–9
36 John 5:28–29
37 Matthew 25:31–46
38 Matthew 25:41–43

6

The Teaching of Jesus about God and Ourselves

If you want to compare various religions, the best way to start is to look at what they believe about God, and then at what they believe about people. You will find that the whole structure of a religion depends upon those two sets of beliefs. Jesus' teaching is no exception.

Jesus' belief and teaching about God was shaped by his knowledge of the Old Testament. So to understand what he meant when he used the word 'God' you must go right back into the Old Testament and become familiar with books such as the Psalms and the writings of the prophet Isaiah. Here we are simply going to underline certain key points in Jesus' teaching about God which occur again and again.

What Jesus taught about God

God is one Like the rest of the Jews, Jesus passionately believed there is only one God — he was a monotheist. Once one of the teachers of Jewish law asked Jesus which was the greatest of God's commandments.[1]

'The most important one,' answered Jesus, 'is this: "Hear, O Israel, the Lord our God, the Lord is one. Love the Lord your God with all your heart and with all your soul and with all your mind and with all your strength".'

The most important commandment to Jesus was that God is one, and that we must love the one, true God with everything we have. Nothing can be added or subtracted from the unity of God. God has no partners.

The God that Jesus talked about was the same God that the great prophets of former centuries had proclaimed. As Jesus once said, this God was 'the God of Abraham, the God of Isaac, and the God of Jacob'.[2]

God is spirit When Jesus was talking to the Samaritan woman at the well, he told her, 'God is spirit, and his worshippers must worship in spirit and in truth.'[3]

God has no physical form. He is outside space and time. He is not restricted by anything.

'No one has ever seen God.'[4]

The only way to worship the one true God is 'in spirit' *and* 'in truth'. Worship must be with all our heart, soul and mind. Many seek to worship God in this way. But do they always worship him 'in truth'?

God is all-powerful 'With God all things are possible,'[5] said Jesus.

Nothing can stop his plan. Nothing can prevent the ultimate triumph of his kingdom — his reign and authority. He is the one universal God of the whole creation.

God is totally good 'No one is good', said Jesus, 'except God alone.'[6]

When Jesus said that God is good, he meant that he is totally good. No evil intent or action can ever come from him. He can never lead someone astray or prevent someone from finding the truth if that person is anxious to find him. He is never a malicious or capricious God who is inconsistent in his character or his dealings with people.

So, contrary to much popular thought at his time, Jesus taught that the general blessings of God in creation were equally available to all people: 'God causes his sun to rise on the evil and the good, and sends rain on the righteous and unrighteous.'[7]

God's goodness in the sense of provision for daily needs was not limited only to those who obeyed him.

At the same time the accidents and suffering of daily life cannot be seen as some 'punishment' sent by God upon some people. We have already seen the automatic reaction of the disciples of Jesus when they saw a man who had been blind from birth: 'Who sinned, this man or his parents, that he was born blind?'[8]

But Jesus stated very clearly that the blindness was not due to the man's sin, nor to that of his parents.

On another occasion some people started telling Jesus one of the local stories that was obviously going around at the time. It was about some people from Galilee who had apparently been killed by Pilate, who was then governor of Palestine, and their blood mixed with that of animal sacrifices.[9] Since Jesus was also from Galilee, they were perhaps trying to frighten him into silence! But Jesus used their talk to drive home a crucial point.

'Do you think that these Galileans were worse sinners than all the other Galileans because they suffered in this way? I tell you, no! But unless you repent, you too will all perish.'

Then Jesus went on to cap their story with another.

'Or those eighteen who died when the tower in Siloam fell on them — do you think they were more guilty than all the others living in Jerusalem? I tell you, no! But unless you repent, you too will all perish.'

God is totally good. He is never the God who sends some random punishment on a group of people just because they happen to be in the wrong place at the wrong time. His goodness is for all types of people, just as human evil and stupidity affects all types of people also . . .

God is like a heavenly Father Even if you have read only a few pages of the New Testament, it will surely have struck you how often God is referred to as 'Father'. And you may have found this rather shocking. What does it really imply?

The only way we can understand a word is by its usage, and not by its usage anywhere, at any time, but its usage in the particular historical and cultural context that we are examining. So we must obviously ask as our first question: Were the Jews before the time of Jesus in the habit of calling God their 'Father'? And, if so, what did they mean to say by using such an expression?

When we look into the Old Testament, we find that there are a number of places in which God is indeed called 'Father'. These examples are especially found in the Psalms of David and in the writings of the great prophets Isaiah and Jeremiah. The term 'Father' is mainly used when emphasizing God's care and compassion. For example, this is how King David sometimes talked about God:

'A father to the fatherless, a defender of widows, is God in his holy dwelling.'[10]

'As a father has compassion on his children, so the Lord has compassion on those who fear him.'[11]

In another Psalm, as someone who is rejoicing in the goodness and protection of God, he prays, 'You are my Father, my God, the Rock my Saviour.'[12]

Isaiah the prophet also cried out to God in prayer:

O Lord, you are our Father.
We are the clay, you are the potter;
we are all the work of your hand.[13]

So the use of the word 'Father' for God was familiar to the Jews before Jesus came. But it was perhaps not the first term that they would have used for prayer or for talking about God. They preferred the more distant terms 'Lord' and 'Creator God'. What Jesus did was to take a term already in use and fill the word with new content and meaning.

Of course it is perfectly clear that the Jews had no idea of giving some physical form to God when they called him 'Father'. This would have been absolute blasphemy, forbidden by the second of the Ten Commandments.[14] They used the term 'Father' because it expressed so much of the love and compassion of the one true God for those who were in need of his care, such as orphans, widows and children. It is a loving Father who holds the clay in his hands and who moulds us — not some distant malicious being that we cannot trust with the shape of our lives.

All language is inadequate when we come to talk about God. We all know that God is so above and beyond our human understanding, that his power and brightness are so infinite compared to our puny powers, that his love and compassion are so deep in contrast to our fickle human emotions — that all our words are very limited expressions of who he is. But the only words that we have to use are human words — and like all other words, these act as models of reality, they are not the reality itself.

Scientists are very used to using models. DNA is the chemical which embodies genetic information. When its double-helical structure was being worked out in the early 1950s, it was by the building of models that the conceptual breakthroughs came. So now we can look at beautiful models of DNA in our laboratories, made up of different-coloured plastic balls. They certainly help us to understand the structure and function of DNA. But everybody knows that the model is not the thing itself! Everybody knows that a molecule of DNA would not *really* look like that if you, say, had the chance to be a mini-electron microscope sitting just inside the nucleus of a cell and looking at it.

The value of models is that they help us to understand something about a reality outside our normal daily experience. It is the same with the terms that we use for God.

Jesus probably used the term 'Father' for the same reasons that it was used in the Old Testament — because it expressed the individual love and care that God had for people. God was not the cold, legalistic, disapproving, distant being that the Pharisees and Sadducees made him out to be. No, he was 'nearer than our jugular vein', someone who was always watching and caring for his children.

So Jesus taught his disciples to pray, '*Our Father* in heaven . . .'[15]

There was nothing disrespectful in this form of prayer. Just to make quite sure that full honour and respect was being given to the one true God, Jesus underlines here, as many places elsewhere, that their Father was *in heaven*. It was precisely because the only true father was in heaven that Jesus refused to allow people to call religious leaders by the name 'Father' here on earth. Such usage would devalue the centrality of God as Father.

When Jesus wanted to tell his disciples how valuable they were in the sight of God, he said, 'Are not two sparrows sold for a penny? Yet not one of them will fall to the ground apart from the will of your Father . . . So don't be afraid; you are worth more than many sparrows.'[16]

When Jesus wanted to emphasize God's love and care for small children, he said, 'See that you do not look down on one of these little ones. For I tell you that their angels in heaven always see the face of my Father in heaven.'[17]

It is '*your Father in heaven*', said Jesus to his disciples, who 'causes his sun to rise on the evil and good.'[18]

So the Father-character of God is one of the central themes in the teachings of Jesus. But apart from being the Creator of all mankind, he is not 'Father' in some vague all-inclusive sense for all people everywhere. 'The Fatherhood of God for mankind' is not something that was taught by Jesus, though the idea has been made popular by others. God as Father is a 'model' only relevant for those who believe in him and obey his commandments. You will look in vain in the teachings of Jesus for any place where it says that God is the Father of those who hate and reject him, or of those who do not reflect his holiness.

For is it not the task of the children of the kingdom to be like their heavenly Father?

God is holy One of the great themes which runs throughout the Old Testament is the theme of the holiness of God. It is a theme which is continued by Jesus, who was vitally concerned to see that people understood what God's holiness really meant.

You can often discover a lot about a person if any of his public prayers have been recorded. Fortunately for us one of the prayers of Jesus has been written down, no doubt as a small group of his disciples were present with him when he prayed.[19] We read that Jesus prayed in a very direct way to his 'Holy Father'[20] and to his 'righteous Father'.[21] The greatest way in which he could show respect in prayer was by underlining the holiness of God.

But when Jesus talked about God being 'holy', he meant something very different from what many people think of as God's 'holiness'. Jesus was not just saying that God is very *different* from ordinary humans, though that is of course true. Nor was he just saying that God is very 'distant' from us and 'apart' from us, though there is great truth in that idea also. No, if we go into the idea of 'holiness' in the Old Testament, it is clear that Jesus was saying that God is a totally-blinding purity. His 'holiness' referred to his specific and consistent opposition to *all* evil and *all* sin of any kind. Trying to bring any hint of sin, impurity or unholiness into his presence is as impossible as mixing oil and water. You may as well try to throw black lumps of coal into the sun and not let them burn.

Just what God's holiness means in practice we have seen very clearly in the teachings of Jesus about God's kingdom in the Sermon on the Mount. It is absolutely clear that the standards which God sets for his kingdom are way above the mere keeping of certain religious laws and rituals. They are standards which take into account our hearts' motivations. They are standards which demand all that we have and are. The standards of the kingdom, in fact, reflect very precisely the character of the King.

For this is what the kingdom of God is all about — being like the King.

So Jesus said, 'You have heard that it was said, "Love your neighbour and hate your enemy". But I tell you, love your enemies and pray for those who persecute you, that you may be sons of your Father in heaven.'[22]

What does Jesus mean here when he talks about being 'sons of your Father'? Is he talking about some physical relationship? Do not misunderstand a vivid metaphor. Do not confuse the model with the reality that the model is trying to express. A son is like his father. He tends to share the same character — at least if he is a good son. Here Jesus is saying that people who enter the kingdom of God should be like good sons of the King. They should share his interests, his character, his holiness. The standards of the kingdom of God are nothing less (and nothing more) than the plumb-line of God's holiness.

Jesus finishes the passage we quoted above with an astonishing statement: 'Be perfect, therefore, as your heavenly Father is perfect.'[23]

Jesus actually commanded those who wanted to enter the kingdom of God to be perfect! But surely this is too idealistic? A nice idea, but not very practical. Good teaching for dreamers, but not for hard-headed men and women like us who have to live in the real world. Surely it is impossible for us to achieve?

It *is* impossible for us to achieve. That is just the point. The Sermon on the Mount is like telling a child at the bottom of Mount Everest to climb to the top. The glaring white peak wreathed in clouds far above him is impressive, an incredible challenge, but quite impractical to reach on his own. Unless, of course, somebody comes to help . . .

God is love If there is one characteristic that singles out the teaching of Jesus about God from all other teachings, then it is his emphasis on God's love. One reason that he spoke out against the religious leaders was that they 'neglected justice *and the love of God*'.[24] They were condemned because they were not *practising* the love of God.[24]

It is a mistake that many make today. They may see God as a defender of their just cause. They may see him as a champion of their human rights. They may even see him as a protector of their community or country, or as an upholder of their hard-won revolution. But do they see him as love? Are they practising his love? If not, then they stand condemned also.

Jesus said that 'God so loved the *world . . .*'[25] The word 'world' here is not referring to the physical created world, but to the world of people. God loves all people — black people, white people, yellow people, people with high IQ and people with low IQ, the privileged and underprivileged, the fat and the thin, the healthy and the sick, the young and the old — God loves them all. He made them all. He longs for all of them to enter his kingdom, to accept his reign.

To drive this message home, Jesus once told a story about a shepherd who had a hundred sheep.[26] One of them wandered away, so the shepherd went off looking and looking for the one who was lost. When he finally found it, he was more happy about that one sheep that was found than about the ninety-nine sheep that were never lost in the first place.

'In the same way', concluded Jesus, 'your Father in heaven is not willing that any of these little ones (children) should be lost.'

God's love is not something passive, but dynamic, active, taking the initiative to reach out to people and meet their deepest needs — if only they are willing. As Jesus said, 'Greater love has no one than this, that one lay down his life for his friends.'[27]

God does not want anyone to be 'lost', but love never forces. It is we who need to respond to his love. And our response means that we will experience and practise his love.

'A new commandment I give you', said Jesus to his disciples. 'Love one another. As I have loved you, so you must love one another. All men will know that you are my disciples if you love one another.'[28]

This is the crucial test of whether someone is a true follower of Jesus or not. If they are not showing any signs of real love in their lives, then you can be sure that they have never really become part of God's kingdom.

God is all-knowing Jesus told his disciples, 'Your Father knows what you need before you ask him.'[29]

God knows everything. Nothing can be hidden from him. There is no way we can think evil thoughts or do evil acts and not be seen.

Even before we pray, God knows exactly what we are going to pray. So what, you might ask, is the point of praying?

Prayer is a rope with many strands. There is the strand of worship and the strand of confession. There is also the strand of asking God for things, or petition. The point of petition is not that God does not know what we need already, but rather that he wants us to express verbally our utter dependence on him. Asking things from our Father in heaven is as natural as a child asking things from his earthly father. It expresses a relationship. It is part of knowing God.

Knowing God? Is that what we just said? Yes, according to Jesus, God can actually be known. But what does that mean? It will take a little while to explain.

God is a knowable God Right at the beginning of Jesus' prayer that we quoted above, and which we find in John chapter 17, Jesus prayed to his heavenly Father, 'Now this is eternal life: that they (his disciples) may know you, the only true God, and Jesus Christ whom you have sent.'[30]

Jesus is saying here that the essence of eternal life is not that it never ends, but rather that it consists of *knowing God*.

But is that not a blasphemous statement? How can an all-powerful, holy, all-knowing Creator God be known by weak and limited human beings?

First, the phrase 'knowing God' here does not imply any physical relationship. This kind of 'knowing' is obviously of a different kind and quality than that which exists between two humans. God is spirit. Man is physical. So this 'knowing' must be a spiritual knowing. We cannot see God, nor can we touch him. However, there are enough similarities between 'physical knowing' and 'spiritual knowing' for the same word 'knowing' to have some real content. If there were no similarities then we would have to find another word!

For example, in spiritual knowing we can speak to God. This is called prayer. God can also speak to us — through his prophets, through the Holy Writings, through our consciences, and sometimes in special ways such as dreams and visions. So there can be two-way communication between us and God. Communication is an essential part of 'knowing'.

Another aspect of 'knowing' is understanding. When we meet another person in 'physical knowing', then we begin to understand him in a way that we never could before. Of course that understanding is never complete — we can never know another person completely, though we may feel that we come very close. In 'spiritual knowing' there is understanding also, except that in this case God knows us through and through, as if we were made of crystal-clear glass, whereas we can only understand him in a very limited way, at least in this life.

A further part of 'knowing' is appreciation. As you get to know someone in 'physical knowing', so you learn how to appreciate that person in a deeper way. Even before 'spiritual knowing' ever begins, God has already shown how much he loves us and cares for us. When we come to know him and we experience his *agape*, self-giving love, in a deeper way, then we learn to appreciate him more as the central focus of our lives. That appreciation is expressed in worship and in making very sure that his kingdom is our highest priority.

There are many other comparisons that we could make between 'physical knowing' and 'spiritual knowing', but I hope that these are sufficient for us to see that there are enough similarities between the two kinds of knowing to make the concept of 'knowing God' far more possible than we may have first thought.

After all, if we are willing to see that God can be our heavenly Father, and we are ready to be the children of his kingdom, then does it seem so strange that the children of the kingdom should know their heavenly Father?

What Jesus taught about people

A good doctor never proceeds with therapy unless he is sure

about his diagnosis. There are many philosophies and religions today which claim to make a correct diagnosis of the human dilemma. That mankind *has* a dilemma is fairly self-evident for those who read their newspapers, let alone travel the world a little.

But what *are* the root causes of his dilemma? And what kind of dilemma is it? Have a few million years of evolution left us with a bundle of genes which make us accident-prone to wars, violence, greed and selfishness? Or what?

The diagnosis of Jesus, like all his other teaching, is radical, and is quite different from the analysis that we find in any other philosophy or religious system.

The world is a disaster area These are not quite the words of Jesus, but they express something that he taught more by his actions than by his words. Jesus had a very vivid sense of the presence of evil in the world and of satanic opposition to the forces of good. From his confrontation with Satan in the wilderness, right on through his public ministry, Jesus moved like a bright light making the darkness around him seem blacker than ever before.

Jesus never saw the world as a kind of morally-neutral area, in which people are born like clean slates and then proceed to 'write' either a good life or a bad life on their slates by their actions. Instead, he saw the whole of the human race as being in the grip of Satan's power. It was as if there had been some giant nuclear disaster in a previous age, and the dreaded fallout of evil, sin and selfishness was still destroying individuals, families, communities and nations.

So it was hardly surprising that the proclamation of the kingdom of God received such satanic opposition. The demons cast out by Jesus and his disciples had no difficulty in recognizing the authority of the kingdom. When the seventy disciples sent out by Jesus to heal and to preach returned from their travels, they reported that even the demons had been in submission.

On hearing this, Jesus said, 'I saw Satan fall like lightning from heaven.'[31]

In other words, as the power of God's kingdom was experienced in people's lives, so Satan's 'kingdom' or authority was being broken down.

When Jesus saw a hunchbacked woman in the synagogue who had been in that condition for eighteen years, he said that it was *Satan* who had kept her bound in that condition.[32] When he healed her, she was not just set free from her illness, but also from her bondage to Satan's power.

As Jesus drew to the end climax of his public ministry, he had this great sense that the final confrontation with Satan was approaching. 'Now the prince of this world will be driven out.'[33]

He saw Satan as a prince, taking for himself the power and authority which rightfully belonged to God alone. There was no possible coexistence between God's power and Satan's power.

How we perceive the world makes a lot of difference as to how we spend our lives. It also affects how we view the various solutions put forward to solve the problems of the human race. If you believe that a sick person has a fairly mild disease, then you will be content with a fairly mild medicine to cure it. But if you know that someone has a potentially fatal disease, then you will be ready for some far more drastic remedies.

Jesus showed that the cancer of sin has affected everyone without exception. The world is a disaster area because the terrible results of that cancer have permeated man's institutions, his relationships, his philosophies and right into his very soul.

There is only one way to overcome one power, and that is to find another power which is greater . . .

The real problem is within us The idea that our basic problem is our environment remains very popular. According to this view, what we really need to do to solve human problems is to improve the environment and this will eventually bring about fundamental changes in people themselves. The problem with this view is that it does not work in practice.

Now there is nothing wrong in attacking the problems we see in our environment. Indeed that is a responsibility for anyone who claims to have anything to do with true submission to God. But let us not be naive and think that mere alterations in the environment are going to change human nature.

There used to be a view that improving health care would eventually lead to the 'new man' — a healthy, robust creature who would jog happily through life, fortified with the right vitamins and health foods, living for longer and longer as the human genetic stock improved.

It is certainly nice to be healthy, and to have the right medical care when one is sick. But the countries where health care is most advanced also have some of the most selfish people, whose only concern seems to be in the fitness of their own bodies. In fact, many even make their own bodies into their own mini-gods. They are so taken up with their own health that there is hardly any time to care for anyone else's. And when their health breaks down, their whole selfish little world collapses with them.

Education is another great factor that many see as leading to the new man and the new society. Who would be against education? Especially if it teaches people how to think critically rather than just learning facts by heart . . . But even educating people to think critically, valuable as that may be, does not seem to tackle the roots of basic human problems. Some of the most educated men in the world have also been the most cruel and most selfish. Well-educated people have sent millions of their fellow human beings to extermination camps. Conversely, there are plenty of people around who have had hardly any education, but who have the most pleasant, kind and unselfish personalities that you can imagine, and a genuine sense of responsibility for society around them.

Certainly crime rates do not seem to have dropped markedly as the level of education in developing countries has increased. Rather, the opposite seems to be the case. And what about alcoholism, drug addiction and the breakup of families? Does improved education make such things disappear from society? Of course we can always escape from the net and say that it is all a question of the right kind of education. But people have been saying this for hundreds of years without making very much difference.

Revolutions are a way advocated by some as leading to fundamental changes in human nature, though the word 'revolution' has been used for so many varied events in recent history that the word itself has lost much of its meaning. But what is so striking about the various kinds of upheavals in societies which are labelled 'revolution' is how similar post-revolution people are to pre-revolution people. If there was a dictatorial regime before the revolution, then the chances of a dictatorial regime taking its place will be very high. Of course the people newly in power will represent different views from the people they had opposed, but after the initial euphoria has worn off, it is very likely that the same old pre-revolutionary problems will begin to appear again. The reason is simply that the people have not changed. Institutions may have changed, the government may have changed, the very face of society may have changed — but the people are the same.

It is rather like having your skin infected with a fungus. You put on the right ointment, bandage the wound and within a few days the skin is dramatically healed. So you throw away your bandage and think that everything is fine. But a few weeks later the same tell-tale spots begin to appear on the surface of the skin in just the same place. The fungus never really went away at all. It carried on living under the surface of the skin. Something more drastic than surface remedies is necessary.

Surely, many people say, that drastic remedy comes when people themselves own the means of production and benefit from their labour rather than merely benefitting others. Is this not the key to fulfilment for individuals in societies? There is no doubt that this is a vital point. Economics play an enormous role in determining happiness and misery in societies. But that is not the issue here. The question is — does changing economic relationships actually change people? Do they find basic answers to their deepest needs and problems through economic change? It hardly seems so. Of course it all depends on how we define 'needs and problems'. But as a country becomes more prosperous, it is not always noticeable that people become more caring, more loving, more concerned about the needs of others, less greedy, selfish and power-hungry. Economic changes are the answer to some huge problems — but they are not the answer to *the* problem: that of human nature.

That is where Jesus focused his diagnosis. It is we who make our environment, not our environment which makes us. We have already quoted the words of Jesus which get to the heart of the matter: 'what comes *out* of man is what makes him "unclean" . . ."[34] The problem is within. Putting right the external influences by education, health care and so on is not a radical enough solution. This is where Marxism is simply not radical enough. Changing social conditions does not change the *heart* of the person, the innermost being, the root cause of sin and evil.

Another time Jesus said, 'Make a tree good and its fruit will be good, or make a tree bad and its fruit will be bad, for a tree is recognized by its fruit . . . Out of the overflow of the heart the mouth speaks. A good man brings things out of the good stored up in him, and the evil man brings evil things out of the evil stored up in him.'[35]

The problem with man is how to change his 'roots' so that his 'fruits' will be different. When people talk about the basic problems of man they often confuse the roots and the fruits.

What is so puzzling about us is our incredible capacity for both good and evil. If you have been brought up in a very sheltered environment, you may think that people are basically nice, and that with a little extra education and encouragement they will become even nicer. You may have wondered why Jesus placed such emphasis on the need to repent in order to receive God's kingdom. Is all this emphasis on our need, our problems, not unduly pessimistic?

If you think like this, I have only one suggestion — take a good look at the world. Travel if you can. Go out and work. Take a look at war. Watch a film of what nuclear weapons do to people. Go to rich, prosperous areas and watch how people behave when they have all they need. Come out from your sheltered existence. Now read carefully the Sermon on the Mount. Look into the recesses of your own heart and see what lies there.

Most people at this particular stage of the twentieth century do not suffer from an overdose of optimism. Many have become totally pessimistic about the human race. They have given up thinking that it has any future and see only the apparent meaninglessness of human existence.

War brings out the two extremes of human potential in very different ways. I have been living through a civil war while writing this book. Much of it has been written against the back-ground noises of the crash of artillery shells and the whoosh of outgoing rockets, the wail of ambulances through the deserted streets and the chatter of automatic gunfire. Sometimes I have been sitting in the corridor for shelter and writing there as shells have started landing close to the house. In the hospital next door, which is where I work, the fruits of man's inhumanity to man are brought daily — the dying restaurant owner with five children, cut down by a sniper's bullet, who was brought in a few days ago; the victims of sudden random shelling, with bodies so torn apart that there is hardly anything to bury; the little children with burnt-out eyes and limbs missing — sometimes so blackened and distorted by a nearby bomb blast that they bear little resemblance to human creatures at all.

Yes, there is plenty in war to help me believe in the truth of Jesus' words. There is something desperately wrong in the human heart. Even animals don't behave like that.

But, ironically, war brings out the best in people as well as the worst. I think of the hundreds of young volunteers in this war who are driving ambulances to take the wounded to hospitals. Many are teenagers. No one told them to help — they simply saw a need and did something. Often they are exposed to incredible risks, taking wounded people to hospital under fire — people whom they do not know and who will never be able to repay them. That is *agape* love — love which expects no reward. I think of our baker's brother, who a few weeks ago went out into the street to help a man who had just been wounded by a shell. A few seconds later another shell exploded and killed him. As far as I know he did not know the wounded man — he just wanted to help.

So people have an extraordinary potential for good as well as for evil. Both are true — often true of the same person at different times. We have probably all experienced times when we did something which we knew to be really good and loving, and other times when we have done things for which we felt (perhaps still feel) thoroughly guilty and ashamed.

Jesus' diagnosis of our problem is neither pessimistic nor optimistic. It is realistic. He is a 'good physician'. It is far better being in the hands of a doctor who tells you the truth than one who tells you what you want to hear. If you have cancer and your doctor tells you that it is a minor problem which needs only an aspirin, your chances of survival are slim. There is no hope without a correct diagnosis. And that is just what Jesus gives to us — a thoroughly realistic analysis of the human dilemma. The diagnosis hurts — especially our pride — but then real truth always hurts.

We are slaves to sin Jesus talked a lot about slavery and freedom. At one time he said, 'I tell you the truth, everyone who sins is a slave to sin.'[36]

Generally people do not like being called slaves to anything — especially if they feel that they are free. Those who listened to Jesus were no exception. But what did Jesus really mean when he talked about being a *slave* to sin? And what did he mean by the word 'sin' anyway?

There are plenty of different ideas of what the word 'sin' means. Some people use the word in a rather cynical, half-amused way to refer to things that modern people no longer need to worry about.

Others use it in a more social context to refer to the various evils or 'sins' of society. There is no doubt that they have a point. There is certainly such a thing as community sin — social evils such as neglect for the poor, racialism, suppression of minorities, and so on.

For yet others 'sin' means breaking the laws of their religion. For example, if they are told to pray so many times every day, and they do not, then this is 'sin'. But generally people do not worry very much about such kinds of 'sin', because they satisfy their consciences with all kinds of good reasons why practising such things is impossible anyway. For example, we are living in a modern, busy world and there is just not time to keep up with all these rituals. And anyway, God understands our situation and realizes that we cannot do everything . . .

But these same people would probably recognize other kinds of major 'sins' in their religions which should certainly be avoided — things such as murder, adultery, theft, or blasphemy against the name of God. So avoiding 'sin', according to this view, is seen mainly as avoiding certain major crimes against other people or against God. Providing you do not do such things, then you have little really to worry about in your religion, whether you actually

practise that religion in other ways or not. So 'sin' is defined
according to what we do not do, rather than according to what we
do.

The teaching of Jesus about sin is different from these various
concepts of 'sin' that we have been examining. His concept of sin
depended far more on the Old Testament writings. For example,
in one of his psalms, David wrote:

Surely I have been a sinner from birth.
Sinful from the time my mother conceived me.[37]

The concept expressed here is quite different from the idea that
everybody is born like a 'clean slate'. This passage from the Old
Testament, which for Jesus was the starting point of all his
teachings, suggests that something is wrong with people right
from the beginning of their lives. The 'cancer of sin' is passed on
from generation to generation, like the oncogene for physical
cancer which we have been using as an illustration since chapter
two. Of course, the inheritance of this built-in tendency to sin is
not a genetic inheritance. It is not the mechanism involved which
is important, but the basic accuracy of the observation.

Do we need schools to teach children how to be bad? I have not
heard of any. Do we need to give our children teaching in the
home about what 'being bad' means? Somehow they seem to
know already. And if you still believe that basically people are
born good and that they only become mean, rebellious, selfish
and unloving much later, then I suggest that you wait until you
have children of your own . . .

So the teaching that every person starts out life with the
tendency towards sin certainly fits with what we observe in
practice. We are not responsible for the tendency itself — how
could we be? But we *are* responsible for our own thoughts and
actions. It is almost as if everybody, in every lifetime, repeats that
great fall of their ancestor Adam.[38]

Jesus saw sin as something rooted in the very nature of human
beings, not just as individual acts of sin. What is this sin in our
natures? It is the fact that we naturally put our own selves, our
own wishes, our own plans and our own self-importance in the
middle of our lives, right in the place where God should have the
central place. If true worship is putting God first in our lives, then

sin is just the opposite — the putting of our egos first.

In fact that is what breaking the first commandment is all about: 'You shall have no other gods apart from me.'[39]

'Sin' means exactly that — the fact that we *do* have other gods besides God — and the number one god in our lives is our own selves. A god is anyone or anything that comes in the place of the one true God.

You may remember how the rich young ruler mentioned in chapter five had to learn about the first commandment the hard way. It was only when Jesus started talking about the man's own self-centred riches that he began to understand what Jesus really meant.

When we begin to understand that worship is the opposite of sin, then we will begin to see the significance of much of the teaching of Jesus on the kingdom of God. When God really reigns in our lives, then that is true worship. Worship means putting God first. So anything which puts God in second place (or lower) is opposite to worship and is therefore sin. That is why Jesus preached that the kingdom of God demands all we have. The religious people must give up their hypocrisy. The rich must let go of their riches. The proud must be humbled. Those who judge others wrongfully must give up their own justice. God must have first place, and since he is a holy God we can only worship him properly if we are holy too.

There are many ways in which we can try to avoid the teaching of Jesus about sin. For example, if we do not believe in God at all, then there is no problem — the very concept of sin ceases to have any meaning at all. The word 'sin' only has meaning when we have an absolute standard or reference point against which to measure our lives. For Jesus that standard was the holiness of God himself. Take away the standard and we are like a builder who tries to build a house with upright walls but has no plumb-line against which to measure them. Or we are like people trying to play a game of football in which no one has first agreed on the rules and for which there is no referee.

It is interesting to note how many people stop believing in God after having done something which they know is opposite to God's holiness. Avoiding responsibility by denying that it exists is a very common human escape route.

Another way to try to avoid the teaching of Jesus about sin is to define the concept for your own convenience. Whether they realize it or not, most people do this. They mentally construct for their own lives a kind of code. It is usually an odd mixture of religious beliefs, pop psychology and common sense, with a strong emphasis on what their particular country or community accepts as normal social behaviour. When such a person hears the word 'sin', they automatically switch off, because they feel quite happy and contented that they are 'keeping to their code'.

You often find people who will say: 'Oh, I've never done anything wrong', or even 'Well, I'm not a sinner.' But when you hear what their particular code of conduct is, it is set so low that anybody but a complete idiot would be able to achieve it!

Yet most of us experience this strange sense of 'falling short' of our goals. Few honest people can say that they actually do all the good things that they set out to do. We all know what is the right thing to do, but so often we fail to achieve it.[40]

So when Jesus talked about being a 'slave to sin', he was referring to this very real experience that we have all had of being unable to worship God as we should, of our inability to put him at the centre of our lives. We are slaves because we do not seem to be able to do anything about it in our own strength. We are like people trying to pull ourselves up in the air using our own shoelaces. We can struggle all we like, but the more we struggle, the more we seem to sink.

If you do not believe that you are a slave to sin, then I suggest that you go back to the teaching of Jesus in the Sermon on the Mount.[41] The practice of that teaching is what true worship is all about. By placing the searchlight of the moral demands of God's kingdom on our lives, all our little codes crumble, all our pathetic excuses fade away, and we are left naked before a holy God, unable to break out of the pattern of our own selfish desires.

As we struggle to find new and different ways to pull ourselves out of our dilemma by our own efforts and religious observances, we are rather like a man in a story who decided to try to reach the sun. Since the sun was very high up, it seemed a logical first step to climb the highest local mountain to see if he was any closer. So that is what he did, but when he reached the summit the sun certainly seemed to be just as far away as before. He decided that the obvious thing to do would be to climb another much higher mountain. He went to eastern Turkey, which was a little distance away, and climbed Mt Ararat. That is a very high and beautiful mountain. It took him a lot of energy and effort to climb it. But when he reached the top, apart from the breathtaking view, it was a very disappointing experience, because when he looked up, the sun still seemed as far away as ever before. However, the man was not so easily put off. Why not climb Mt Everest! As the highest mountain in the world, that would surely bring him closer to the sun . . .

So the man got together a large expedition and spent a lot of money and time on his climb of Mt Everest. He had a tremendous sense of exhilaration when he finally reached the summit and planted there his very own expedition flag. But when he looked up, it was a bitter blow — through the mist and the clouds it was obvious that the sun was just as far away.

Such is the foolishness of the person who thinks he will reach God by his own efforts and religious observances. We are slaves to sin. Let us face the facts.

Man's amazing potential If we finish the chapter on that note, you would rightfully accuse Jesus of being a gloomy pessimist. But that is not the end of the story.

Jesus made it very clear that freedom from slavery was possible. More by his acts than by his teaching he demonstrated that God's kingdom was breaking into the present evil age to set people free. No one was beyond the point of being set free by God. However far gone they were, however corrupt, however selfish, however cruel, however anti-religious even, there was still hope.

That is another reason why Jesus had so much time for outcasts. God's kingdom was available for all. Once there were two blind men who heard that Jesus was passing nearby.[42] So they both started shouting out, 'Lord, Son of David, have mercy on us!'

The crowd around Jesus told them to shut up because they were making so much noise. But they just shouted louder than before! Jesus pushed his way right through the crowd to where the noise was coming from and asked them what they wanted.

'We want our sight', they said.

So Jesus had compassion on them and healed their eyes.

Jesus is for the people on the edge of the crowd. He is for the ones that no one else is willing to listen to. Nobody is potentially beyond the reach of the kingdom of God.

The teaching of Jesus is about God and about people; holy God and sinful people; the impossibility of pulling ourselves out of the human dilemma and coming to know God by our own efforts.

You may be forgiven for thinking that the teaching of Jesus has placed us in an apparently impossible dilemma. We seem to be in a dark underground prison with heavily-locked doors, so far from the freedom of the bright sunshine above. Doesn't anyone have the key?

Do you believe in a great, almighty Creator God? 'With God all things are possible.'

1   Mark 12:29
2   Mark 12:26
3   John 4:24
4   John 1:18
5   Matthew 19:26
6   Luke 18:19
7   Matthew 5:45
8   John 9:2–3
9   Luke 13:1–5
10 Psalm 68:5
11 Psalm 103:13
12 Psalm 89:26
13 Isaiah 64:8
14 Exodus 20:4–5
15 Matthew 6:9
16 Matthew 10:29–30
17 Matthew 18:10
18 Matthew 5:45
19 John 17
20 John 17:11
21 John 17:25
22 Matthew 5:43

23 Matthew 5:48
24 Luke 11:42
25 John 3:16
26 Matthew 18:12–14
27 John 15:13
28 John 13:34–35
29 Matthew 6:8
30 John 17:3
31 Luke 10:18
32 Luke 13:16
33 John 12:31; see also John 14:30; 16:11
34 Mark 7:20–23
35 Matthew 12:33–35
36 John 8:34
37 Psalm 51:5
38 If you are interested in reading what the Bible teaches us about the fall of man, look at Genesis 3:1–19
39 Exodus 20:3
40 There is a fascinating account by one of the early followers of Jesus about his personal experience on this subject of 'falling short'. It is found in Romans 7.
41 Matthew 5 – 7
42 Matthew 20:29–34

7

Four gospels or one?

Before we consider how the disciples viewed the claims of Jesus, we must first briefly examine a crucial question. How do we know that the New Testament we have today is the same as the original New Testament written down in the first century? We may be willing to accept what the New Testament tells us are the teachings of Jesus about love, social justice and helping the poor. But when we come to look in the next chapter at the claims of Jesus, they are so extraordinary and shocking that we might be tempted to believe that the disciples of Jesus made them up. How can we know that the New Testament we have today gives us the original teachings of Jesus?

A corrupted New Testament?

According to one view, the New Testament, or Injil, was a holy book which was revealed from heaven to Jesus, probably by means of an angel, and which he then wrote down. However, in later years, Christian priests corrupted the original text and changed parts, especially those which relate to the claims of Jesus. Because of this, several contradictory 'New Testaments' began to circulate. The priests therefore had a problem. Which should they accept as the true one? To solve the problem they decided to have a big church council which some claim was the council at Iznik (Nicea). This took place in AD 325. During this council, so the story goes, they chose one as the true New Testament and burnt all the other copies.

Another version of the story is that at this council they chose 'four Gospels' which they published as one book, and that these are what Christians read today, although these four contradict each other.

The first point of confusion in the story concerns the fact that the New Testament we have today certainly contains four accounts of the life and teachings of Jesus, known as the four 'Gospels'. These are the accounts that we have been using as the main source material throughout this book. They are named after the four men who wrote them — Matthew, Mark, Luke and John. Two of these, Matthew and John, were from the twelve disciples of Jesus. Mark was a young man living in Jerusalem while Jesus was carrying out his public ministry and who saw many of the things that Jesus did.

Luke was a non-Jewish physician from Antioch (Antakya in modern Turkey). He was also a very careful historian who laid great stress on the accuracy of his life of Jesus. He originally wrote his account for one particular follower of Jesus called Theophilus, but later on his account came into general circulation. It is interesting to read the introduction that Luke gives to his account:[1]

> Many have undertaken to draw up an account of the things that have been fulfilled among us, just as they were handed down to us by those who from the first were eye-witnesses and servants of the word. Therefore, *since I myself have carefully investigated everything from the beginning*, it seemed good also to me to write an orderly account for you, most excellent Theophilus, so *that you may know the certainty of the things you have been taught*.

So Luke wrote with a specific purpose in mind — to carry out a careful investigation into the life of Jesus using firsthand reports and depending on eyewitnesses of the events.

Each of the four accounts of Jesus was written for a specific readership. Matthew was writing particularly with Jews in mind, so he includes a lot of material which would have been of particular interest to Jews. As a tax-collector, he would have been used to recording accurate details. He would quite likely have kept careful records of what Jesus did and taught as he lived with him for the three years of his public ministry.

Mark was writing particularly to non-Jewish Roman citizens. In fact, there is some evidence that he was writing in Rome itself. So his account is shorter and more action-packed than the others

— a book for busy city life, focusing mainly on what Jesus *did* rather than on what he taught. There is some evidence that Peter, one of the main disciples of Jesus, had a big hand in the writing of Mark. Peter himself had always been a man of action.

If you compare Matthew, Mark and Luke, you will find that they are very similar. There are two reasons for this. One is that Mark was written first and both Matthew and Luke use his account to write theirs. Since Peter was one of the main disciples, and since Mark's account probably carried his personal eye-witness authority, it is logical that Mark's account should have been used as a prime source. The other reason that Matthew and Luke, in particular, are similar, is that they probably share another common historical source along with Mark's account.

Matthew, Mark and Luke were written during the years AD 40–70, within a few decades of the life of Jesus. Since they clearly depended on earlier written sources, this would push the date of the source material back to just a few years after the public ministry of Jesus.

John's account is quite different in its approach from the other three. This is probably because John wrote his account of Jesus' life quite independently of the others. There is some evidence that he was writing at least some of it in Ephesus (now in Turkey), probably in the last decade of the first century AD. The first part of John's Gospel uses the rather Greek idea of Jesus being the Logos of God, the Word of God. However, his account is also very Jewish in its approach. There is good evidence that John's native language was Aramaic, the everyday language of Jesus himself, because some of the grammatical structures in his account, written in Greek, are Aramaic in form. These are quite easy to detect. When you listen to foreigners speaking your own language you can often notice parts that sound 'funny' because the foreigner is translating word for word from his own language. This happened to John when he was translating the original Aramaic words of Jesus into Greek.

The reason the various accounts were written in Greek is that Greek was the common written language of the Roman Empire. In this way they could circulate widely to a much bigger readership.

When was the New Testament written?

How do we know that these four accounts were written so soon after the life of Jesus himself?

We know that the city of Jerusalem was totally destroyed by the Romans in AD 70. During the course of that destruction many of the main landmarks of the city were obliterated or buried under rubble. However, in all four accounts there are details given of Jerusalem which only an eyewitness of the city could have known. So either the writers had seen these things for themselves or else they were using earlier sources in which these details were given. Either way, the material relating to Jesus in Jerusalem must have come from sources dated before AD 70.

Some very early fragments of the accounts have been discovered. For example, in 1917 a fragment of John's account was discovered in Egypt. It consists of part of John 18, and can be seen in the John Rylands Library in Manchester, England. It dates from AD 130. The text is exactly the same as we have in our New Testaments today. This is very significant, because it means that although John wrote his account in Turkey, it was already circulating in Egypt in AD 130 in a form exactly as we have it today.

The four accounts were quoted from very widely by earlier followers of Jesus during the years AD 90–160. For example, Clement, bishop of Rome, sent a letter in AD 96 to a group of Jesus' followers in the Greek city of Corinth. In the course of this letter he quotes from Matthew, Mark and Luke. Ignatius, bishop of Antioch, was taken to Rome to be executed for his faith in AD 115. As he travelled he wrote several letters in which he quotes from Matthew, John, and many other parts of the New Testament.

In fact, up to the Council of Iznik (Nicea) in AD 325, there are about 32,000 quotations from the writings of the New Testament which may be found in other ancient manuscripts.

The four accounts were used by followers of Jesus at a very early date and were referred to collectively as 'The Gospel', *Euangelion* in Greek, which means 'Good News'. Ignatius, writing his letters mentioned above in the year AD 115, refers to 'The Gospel' (in the singular) as an authoritative writing. By

AD 170 an Assyrian called Tatian had taken the four accounts and used extensive quotations from them to make a kind of selection or harmony of the life and teachings of Jesus.

To give further evidence concerning the early date of the accounts of the life of Jesus is outside the scope of this book. But I hope these examples will gives some idea of just how extensive the data is.

Why four accounts?

But why were four accounts or 'Gospels' written anyway? The answer is simple. If you want a fuller appreciation and understanding of what some historical figure did and said, then it is best to read several biographies about that person. Matthew, Mark, Luke and John are not biographies in the modern sense of the term. Instead they focus deliberately on those periods in the life of Jesus, such as his birth and his public ministry, which will help us to understand why he came.

Each fills out the account of the other so that we obtain a much more complete picture of who Jesus was and what he did. They arranged their material according to their readership. They have differences in emphasis. They are like four TV cameras recording an event. Each cameraman focuses on a slightly different part of the event, or covers a different angle. Because they each have a different picture we do not say they contradict each other. Rather, one complements the others to build up a complete picture of an event.

We would also expect differences of wording between the four accounts when we consider that they are translating original Aramaic passages and conversations into Greek. Different people may translate the same passage with the same meaning, but with a different grammatical structure. At the same time the four writers pick and choose their materials carefully. One may give a story in great detail, another may condense it to a bare outline. But this kind of variation makes no difference to the meaning. In fact, the differences show that the manuscripts are authentic. If all differences had been ironed out to make the different accounts 'look right', we would be rightly suspicious!

Jesus never wrote a book. Instead, his life and teachings were faithfully recorded by these four people soon after his life on earth was over.

And at the same time, other close followers of Jesus, such as Paul, were writing to early communities of Jesus' followers, explaining much of what Jesus taught. These writings were gathered together with the Gospels written by Matthew, Mark, Luke and John into one book during the early part of the second century. It is this book which today is called the 'New Testament'.

Followers of Jesus believe that this book is inspired by God and that God has preserved it from all error. This belief is based on the promise Jesus made to his disciples when he told them, 'The Holy Spirit, whom the Father will send in my name, will teach you all things and will remind you of everything I have said to you.'[2]

The books of the New Testament were equally to be seen as 'God-breathed' (as Paul described it to Timothy) as the Old Testament Scriptures.[3]

And in any case, do we not believe that God is great enough to preserve his holy books? Is God so limited that he cannot preserve his holy New Testament from corruption? If we believe in the one all-powerful Creator God, then we must surely believe that he has kept his books from change all down the years.

But you do not have to believe that the New Testament is inspired by God in order to study the life and teachings of Jesus. If you like, for the moment just take them as a collection of ancient reliable historical manuscripts. But be assured of their reliability. As a scientist I have a rather sceptical temperament and do not believe things easily without sufficient evidence. But, having looked carefully into the matter, I am quite convinced that the New Testament we have today is a trustworthy account of what Jesus said and did.

As for the stories about 'conflicting Gospels' circulating and then many being burnt, there is really no historical evidence for this. I have tried to trace the story back as far as possible, but the earliest written record of it that I have heard of is no earlier than the twelfth century AD, 1,100 years later than the time when the New Testament was first written!

The Council of Iznik (Nicea) did indeed take place in AD 325, but it was not concerned with 'conflicting Gospels'. In fact we have a very full account of this council from the historian Eusebius, who tells us that one of the main aims of the conference was to summarize basic Christian beliefs in a simply memorized form. To this day, the summary is called 'The Nicean Creed'. Eusebius tells us that to make the summary, the council members quoted extensively from the New Testament that was widely circulated by that time.

If anyone believes that the New Testament has been corrupted, then the burden of finding historical proof lies with them. When was it corrupted? By whom? And why? Since many of the early followers of Jesus were executed for their faith, as faith in Jesus was seen as a threat to emperor-worship, why should they deliberately make up a doctrine which they knew would result in their own death? And if the New Testament was changed, how is it we have 32,000 quotations from the New Testament in other writings dating from AD 100–325 which are essentially the same as the passages that we find in the New Testament today?

And if the early church made up part of the story of Jesus because he was a sort of folk-hero to them, how could they have made up teaching as sublime as that of Jesus? The disciples were as surprised at Jesus' teaching, and slow to understand it, as any others. They were not clever spinners of stories or weavers of fables. Many fanciful legends that people tried to pass off as stories of Jesus were rightly rejected: they can be read in so-called 'apocryphal Gospels' which are totally different from the real thing. No: anyone making up the life and teaching of Jesus would have to be as great as Jesus himself to do so. The truth is much more convincing than such speculation.

One last point on this topic. You may have the idea that God's holy books are given to man in a certain language and that to try to translate these books correctly into other languages is impossible. It is true that books often lose something in translation. I am sure that someone reading the New Testament in the original Greek will obtain some shades of meaning which others may not obtain when they read it in another language. However, the loss is not great, and we must not forget that the original teachings of Jesus were given in Aramaic anyway, not in Greek.

If you are someone who believes in one true God who is the God of all nations and all peoples, then I am sure you will have no difficulty in believing that God can speak equally well to all people, whatever their race or language might be. That is why the New Testament has now been translated into more than 590 languages, and portions of it are available in a further 900 languages. God is the God of the whole earth. No race or ethnic group can ever feel superior because the New Testament was originally given in their language. All people are equal in the sight of God.

1   Luke 1:1–4
2   John 14:26
3   2 Timothy 3:16

8

How did the disciples view the claims of Jesus?

We now come to a topic which can lead to misunderstanding. The best way to overcome possible misunderstandings is to try to put ourselves in the place of Jesus' disciples and ask ourselves how we would have considered his extraordinary claims. It is vital to see what Jesus was claiming for himself and what he was not. Sometimes we hear various phrases and think that they mean one thing, when really they mean something quite different. We need to be objective and study the evidence, not just accept stories and tales that we may have heard from others.

We also have to face the fact that we are all prejudiced to some extent by our backgrounds. I know that I have many prejudices from my own background. I can remember hearing when I was small many different stories about what people were like in the Middle East — how they dress, what they believe, how they behave, and so on. Now that I have lived in the Middle East for many years I know that many of these stories are quite false! It is always good to measure our own prejudices against the facts of experience.

I hope you will be willing to do the same as you listen to the claims of Jesus. You may have heard all kinds of stories about what he taught about himself from the time you were a child. So now is the opportunity to review those stories according to the first-hand evidence that we have in the New Testament.

Can God do anything?

For someone who believes in one all-powerful Creator God, this may seem a very curious question to ask. Of course God can do anything! He must be able to by definition. That is what we mean when we talk about 'God'.

The question is a very important one to ask ourselves as we come to consider the claims of Jesus about himself. Sometimes the disciples were not ready enough to listen carefully to his claims because they believed that God would act only in certain ways or do things according to a certain set pattern. We must beware of trying to dictate to God how he should or should not act in this world.

Scientists are rather used to approaching observed phenomena in an open-ended kind of way, so if you are a scientist you may find the task of considering the claims of Jesus a little easier. When scientists do their research, they are supposed to come with an open mind to the data, willing to be persuaded either way as to whether their hypothesis is true or false. The problem often comes because they believe their hypothesis so strongly that they are unwilling to accept the facts that contradict it once they have obtained them! Some of the most interesting advances in science have come because someone has noticed some 'odd' data, observations which do not fit with currently-held dogma.

One important point that should make us especially ready for surprises is that we are talking about claims concerning a revelation from God. We know that it is quite impossible for finite human beings to understand fully the infinite God. We are in time, space and history. Our minds are very limited. God is outside time, space and history. He is totally unlimited by anything. So the 'light' that we have about God in this life will always be very limited compared to the glory of the Light himself. Any knowing that we have will be of a very limited kind, and we can know only as much about God as he chooses to reveal of himself. Certainly we can see much of his power and goodness by looking at the created world around us. But how do we know that God is just, or all-loving, or merciful? Only because he has revealed that to us through his prophets and holy writings. Otherwise we would never have known, for there is no way that we can guess.

When God chooses to reveal himself to us in a particular way, we should certainly not expect that new knowledge about himself to be simple and to fit nicely with our little rules of human logic. God is God! I am always suspicious of people who claim that the character of God is really very 'simple', and that his character may be neatly expressed in a list of characteristics. That list is important, and it is certainly better than having no list at all, but let us not think that we have somehow 'understood' God by reading that list.

Indeed, if your 'God' is a being who can easily be understood by the human mind, then I wonder if he is the one true Creator God at all. If your God is no greater than your mind, then he sounds suspiciously to me like a creation of your own imagination. Surely the One who creates must be above and beyond the one who is created?

Again, scientists are rather accustomed to handling data which at the time seems to be logically contradictory. For example, it is a well-known fact that in physics it is sometimes necessary to picture light as behaving like waves, and at other times like corpuscles or little particles, in order to do justice to the observed behaviour of light. In a sense this is contradictory — light cannot be both waves and particles — but both 'models' are essential to explain the data, and you have to believe both. One day, no doubt, a new model will become available which will make the apparent contradiction disappear.

A well-known example of such an apparent contradiction which occurs in several religions (including the teaching of the Bible), is the idea that God chooses people, but that at the same time they choose God. In the Bible you will find plenty of passages which emphasize the truth of both ideas. Both are true at the same time. By the ordinary laws of our very limited human knowledge, the two ideas are certainly contradictory. One appears to exclude the other. But this is what one should *expect* when looking at the relationships between God and man. We must expect some surprises — it would be strange if there were none. Probably in heaven such apparent contradictions will fade away and, in some different dimension, the problem itself will cease to have any meaning. Is God not great enough to so arrange things that he does indeed choose, but in such a way that man does not lose his free will? The important point is that we are faithful to *all* the data that we have, not excluding some data just because it does not fit with our present very limited concepts.

Having cleared the ground of issues which might otherwise

have held us up, we are now ready to take a look at the disciples of Jesus and of what they thought about the claims of Jesus.

What did the disciples believe?

The twelve disciples of Jesus were typical Jews. In many ways they were more typical than the religious leaders such as the Pharisees and the Sadducees, because they were common workers. They represented the ordinary people of the time. Several of them were conservative Galilean fishermen.

The disciples, like Jesus, were passionate monotheists. They would have been deeply shocked if anyone had challenged this basic belief of their religion — that God is one. If they ever heard of the various gods of Greek mythology, they would certainly have been deeply disgusted. Such beliefs in a whole collection of gods who were born and who died and who fought and killed one another, were totally opposite to all that the Jewish religion stood for.

It is quite probable that most, or all, of the disciples would never have heard of such tales. They were ordinary fishermen, spending many long hours on the Sea of Galilee or by the lakeside mending their nets, not people who had much time for study or for investigating other religions and philosophies.

Galilee was not like our 'global village' in which ideas flow around the world in seconds. It was, by the standards of our day, a cultural isolate. A genetic isolate occurs when a population breeds within itself, so creating a group of people with a similar genetic constitution. Cultural isolates occur when a group of people live very much within their own community in a certain geographical area. Slow population change and limited travel lead to slow cultural change, and the traditions and beliefs of society tend to be handed down relatively unchanged from generation to generation.

Within 500 kilometres of where I am sitting I could take you to visit many such 'cultural isolates', places where time seems to have stood still, where life still continues much as it has done for hundreds of years. And this is with television, videos, radios and newspapers! How much more slowly would different ideas have filtered to the ears of conservative fishermen living in Galilee in first-century Palestine. They were not religious connoisseurs, tasting from all the various ideas that were available in other parts of the empire, but rural Jews, with simple but strongly-held views, highly resistant to change.

Try to imagine, if you can, that you were one of the disciples of Jesus. What would you have observed? In that particular culture, how would you have interpreted what you saw and experienced?

The miracles

Certainly the disciples would have immediately noticed the miracles that Jesus did. From the very beginning of his public ministry Jesus healed the sick and cast out demons. There were probably all kinds of religious people going around at the time who claimed to have miraculous powers, just as there still are in many countries today. But everyone recognized that Jesus was different.

After seeing a demon shake a man and come out of him with a shriek, we read that 'the people were all so amazed that they asked each other, "What is this? A new teaching — and with authority! He even gives orders to evil spirits and they obey him." '[1]

There was a growing recognition among the disciples and the people in general that, because of the miracles he did, Jesus was from God. The disciples put their faith in Jesus because of the very first miracle that he did in Cana in Galilee[2] The crowds followed him because of his miracles.[3] A blind man whose eyes Jesus opened summarized the general belief of the people very clearly: 'If this man were not from God, he could do nothing.'[4]

With their Jewish background, everyone understood that such amazing things could only be done by God himself. So the natural results of such miracles was to bring praise to God. When the blind beggar received his sight, we read that he 'followed Jesus, praising God. When all the people saw it, they also praised God.'[5]

This is why the Pharisees had such a conflict with Jesus when they claimed that the power he obviously had actually came from

Satan. It is an interesting point that even the opponents of Jesus recognized clearly the power and authority which he possessed. It was not the *facts* of the miracles that were in question — everybody could see those for themselves — rather it was the interpretation of the facts that was a matter for debate.

Jesus told them how ridiculous it was to think that he could cast out demons by the power of Satan.[6] That was like Satan casting out the members of his own kingdom, which did not make sense. 'But', said Jesus, 'if I drive out demons by the finger of God, then the kingdom of God has come to you.'

Jesus was not suggesting here that God had any physical form. Rather, he was using a vivid Aramaic metaphor to express the activity of God in his kingdom. His miracles meant that *God* was at work in their midst.

Jesus the prophet

In Jewish history before the time of Jesus, miracles had always been associated with prophets. Moses had done miracles, and so had other prophets such as Elijah. As people saw what Jesus was doing, their natural response was to think he was a prophet.

One day Jesus went to a town called Nain.[7] As he approached the town gate, a dead person was being carried out — the only son of a widow. When Jesus saw her, his heart went out to her and he said, 'Don't cry.' Then he went up and touched the coffin, commanding the dead man to get up. The dead man sat up and began to talk. Listen to the response of the disciples and the crowd: 'They were all filled with awe and praised God. "A great prophet has appeared among us," they said. "God has come to help his people." '

After Jesus miraculously fed the crowd of more than 5,000 people, using five loaves of bread and two small fish, the people said, 'Surely this is the Prophet who is to come into the world.'[8]

The prophet they were referring to here was someone that Moses had said would come: 'The Lord your God will raise up for you a prophet like me from among your own brothers. You must listen to him . . .'[9]

God said of this prophet, 'If anyone does not listen to my words that the prophet speaks in my name, I myself will call him to account.'[9]

When Jesus rode triumphantly into Jerusalem towards the end of his public ministry, the whole city was stirred and asked, 'Who is this?'[10]

The crowd answered, 'This is Jesus, the prophet from Nazareth in Galilee.'

It is clear that Jesus himself accepted that he was a prophet. In one place, referring to his reception in his own home area of Galilee, he pointed out that 'a prophet has no honour in his own country.'[11] Referring to his own imminent death in Jerusalem he said, 'Surely no prophet can die outside Jerusalem!'[12]

Jesus certainly claimed that he was a prophet. But was he more than a prophet?

Jesus forgives sin

One day Jesus was teaching in a house packed with listeners.[13] Some people came carrying a paralyzed man on a mat. They tried to take him into the house to put him in front of Jesus, but this proved impossible because the crowd was so thick. So they went up on the mud roof, made a hole, and let the man down through the hole. At least they showed some initiative!

When Jesus saw their faith, he said to the paralyzed man lying in front of him, 'Friend, your sins are forgiven.'

The man must have been quite shocked to hear the words — but he was not the only person to be shocked. The Jewish leaders who were present started saying to themselves, 'Who is this fellow who speaks blasphemy? Who can forgive sins but God alone?'

Jesus quickly saw what they were thinking, so he asked them, 'Which is easier: to say, "Your sins are forgiven", or to say, "Get up and walk?" But that you may know that the Son of Man has authority on earth to forgive sins . . . He said to the paralyzed man, "I tell you, get up, take your mat and go home." '

Immediately he stood up in front of them, took his mat and went home praising God.

This was no isolated occasion. One evening Jesus was having dinner with Simon, one of the Pharisees.[14] A prostitute came in and began to anoint the feet of Jesus with an expensive jar of perfume that she had brought. The Pharisee was deeply shocked that Jesus should allow such a thing to happen, though washing the feet of a weary traveller when he came to a home for hospitality was a common practice at the time.

So Jesus told the Pharisee a story about two men who owed money to a money-lender. One owed him a lot, the other little. The money-lender decided to cancel both debts. Jesus asked, which of them would love the money-lender most? Simon the Pharisee replied that obviously the one who had the biggest debt cancelled would love most.

Having made his point, Jesus then turned to deal with the woman and said to Simon, 'Do you see this woman? I came into your house. You did not give me any water for my feet, but she wet my feet with her tears and wiped them with her hair . . . therefore, I tell you, her many sins have been forgiven — for she loved much. But he who has been forgiven little loves little.'

Then Jesus told the woman, 'Your sins are forgiven.'

The other guests began to say among themselves, 'Who is this who forgives sins?'

Jesus said to the woman, 'Your faith has saved you; go in peace.'

Jesus' power over nature

We have already seen repeatedly how Jesus had power and authority to heal sick bodies. On several other occasions he showed that he had control over the normal workings of nature as well.

For example, Jesus was once in a small boat with his disciples on the Sea of Galilee.[15] A furious storm blew up and the waves began to sweep over the boat. The disciples panicked and started shouting, 'Lord, save us! We're going to drown!'

Jesus replied, 'You of little faith, why are you so afraid?'

Then he got up, ordered the winds and the waves to stop, and it became completely calm. The disciples were amazed and asked,

'What kind of man is this? Even the winds and the waves obey him!'

Another time Jesus walked on the surface of the water to where the terrified disciples were out in a boat.[16] And on more than one occasion he fed crowds numbering thousands of people by multiplying a few loaves of bread and a few fish.[17]

Jesus as sinless

If you live with someone for a long time, then you will very quickly have a deep awareness of their weak points. Can you imagine living in the same household with a brother, sister, cousin, wife or husband — and then coming to believe after years of observation that one of them was sinless?

The disciples lived with Jesus for three years. They travelled with him everywhere he went. They saw him under stress, at times of opposition and when he was tired and hungry. They had opportunities to meet his mother and members of his own family. So the disciples were in a position to ask them all kinds of interesting questions about what he had done *before* he began preaching and healing people.

Jesus himself claimed that he was sinless. He challenged his listeners one day, 'Can any of you prove me guilty of sin? If I am telling the truth, why don't you believe me?'[18]

It is very easy to *claim* that one is sinless! But what about the proof? The proof must surely lie with the observers — those who can test the claim by their own firsthand experience.

Do not forget the way in which the New Testament uses the word 'sin'. As we saw in the last chapter, sin means far more than breaking certain laws. Peter, one of Jesus' disciples, was a man who understood very fully the real meaning of the word 'sin'. He was the very first of the twelve disciples.[19] He lived with Jesus through the whole time of his public ministry and was with him right to the end. Yet after living and working with Jesus for all this time, Peter could write about him by quoting a verse from the Old Testament:

> He committed no sin,
> and no deceit was found in his mouth.[20]

Another of the early followers of Jesus remarked that Jesus had been 'tempted in every way, just as we are — yet was without sin.'[21]

Most people are very quick to find fault with others, though they find it less easy to see their own faults! It is therefore extraordinary that neither the disciples of Jesus nor even his bitterest enemies were ever able to rightfully accuse him of sin. He was never irritable with people. He never told a lie. He lived out totally in his life the teachings of the Sermon on the Mount. As Jesus himself said during the course of the sermon, 'Do not think that I have come to abolish the Law or the prophets; I have not come to abolish them but to fulfil them.'[22] When Jesus talked about the 'Law' and 'prophets' here he was referring to all the Old Testament writings, including the Ten Commandments.

So Jesus was making the extraordinary claim that he, and he alone, totally fulfilled the Law of God on earth. It was like people gazing for centuries at the misty white peak of Mount Everest, but with no realistic hope that anyone will be able to reach the top. Then one day someone comes along who actually does it, and single-handed they scale the impossible mountain.

Would anyone else be able to follow in the steps of Jesus?

Jesus as the Son of Man

Jesus frequently referred to himself as the 'Son of Man'. In fact, he used this title of himself probably more than any other. What does it mean?

We can only understand such a title by its cultural context and by the way in which it is used.

One point Jesus clearly wanted to drive home in his use of the title was the fact of his own humanity. There is no doubt that Jesus was a human being who shared all the normal pressures of human existence, who became tired and hungry, who was tempted in all the ways in which we are and who experienced to the full what human suffering and pain involves.

There are many places in which Jesus seems to deliberately use the title 'Son of Man' to underline this point. For example, when Jesus was talking about the cost of people following him, especially at a time when he had no fixed home of his own, he said, 'Foxes have holes and birds of the air have nests, but the *Son of Man* has no place to lay his head.'[23]

In another place Jesus was criticizing the way in which the crowds who followed him were so irrational in their opinions.[24] For example, John the Baptist had come as a more traditional Jewish type of prophet, living in the desert and fasting frequently. The people said 'He has a demon'. But, said Jesus, when 'the *Son of Man* came eating and drinking' people began to say 'Here is a glutton and a drunkard, a friend of tax collectors and "sinners".'

So when Jesus was talking about his very ordinary human lifestyle, mixing with people and both giving and receiving hospitality, he deliberately chose the title 'Son of Man'.

Jesus used the title also when he was talking about how he had come to serve others. Once the mother of James and John, two of Jesus' disciples, came to ask Jesus if her sons could have a special place in his kingdom.[25] Perhaps she thought that Jesus was about to become king in Palestine! It was a very natural question. Why not pull a few strings in order to obtain some future benefits?

But Jesus told her and her two sons that true greatness lay in quite a different direction: 'Whoever wants to become great among you must be your servant, and whoever wants to be first must be your slave — just as the *Son of Man* did not come to be served, but to serve, and to give his life as a ransom for many:'

On another occasion, when he washed the feet of his own disciples, Jesus showed how being a leader meant serving others.[26] He also frequently used the term 'Son of Man' when talking about his future suffering.

If you continue to study the various uses of the term 'Son of Man' in the New Testament, you will soon find that Jesus also used the title in another and totally different way.

For example, you may have noticed that in our question above concerning the time when Jesus healed the paralytic, Jesus said to the man, 'But that you may know that the *Son of Man* has authority on earth to forgive sins . . .'[27]

Far from emphasizing his humanity, Jesus is clearly emphasizing his God-given authority.

Even more extraordinary are those many occasions on which Jesus linked the title 'Son of Man' with his own coming again. There are some long sections in the New Testament in which Jesus talks specifically about the signs which will precede the end of the world. We will discuss these in greater detail later.

During one of these teaching-times with his disciples, Jesus said, 'At that time (the end of the world) the sign of the *Son of Man* will appear in the sky, and all the nations of the earth will mourn. They will see the *Son of Man* coming in the clouds of the sky, with power and great glory.'[28]

What is Jesus saying here? Fortunately we know what his Jewish listeners would have understood, because Jesus is quoting directly from a prophecy which is found in the Old Testament and which was probably familiar to most Jews at that time. It was quite possible that Jewish schoolchildren had to learn it by heart during the course of their religious instruction. The prophecy was seen by Daniel in a vision.

> In my vision at night I looked, and there before me was one like a son of man, coming with the clouds of heaven. He approached the Ancient of Days (God) and was led into his presence. He was given authority, glory and sovereign power; all peoples, nations and men of every language worshipped him. His dominion is an everlasting dominion that will not pass away, and his kingdom is one that will never be destroyed.[29]

The term 'Son of Man' in these writings was firmly linked with the glorious figure who would 'come with the clouds of heaven', who would have complete authority over 'all peoples and nations' and who would have an 'everlasting kingdom'.

How can we know that this was indeed the idea that came to the mind of at least some Jews as they listened to Jesus? We can tell by their reactions.

One striking example comes from the time Jesus was on trial, a topic we will cover in more detail in the next chapter. When Jesus was brought before the high priest, with all the teachers of the Law and the elders assembled there — people who would have known the book of Daniel very well — he said, 'I say to all of you: In future you will see the *Son of Man* sitting at the right hand of the Mighty One and coming on the clouds of Heaven.'

On hearing this, the high priest tore his clothes and said, 'He has spoken blasphemy! Why do we need any more witnesses? Look, now you have heard the blasphemy.'[30]

So it is clear from the context that the high priest understood precisely what Jesus was claiming! It was perfectly plain to everyone that Jesus was blaspheming. He was actually saying that he, standing there before them, was some sort of fulfilment of that prophecy made by Daniel all those centuries before. He was also claiming that he was going to fulfil, sometime in the future, the rest of the prophecy — the part about the 'Son of Man' coming on the clouds with glory.

Jesus as the Messiah

Perhaps the best generally-known title for Jesus is the 'Messiah'. In many languages Jesus is known as 'Isa Mesih', 'Jesus the Messiah'. Many people think that 'Mesih' was the family name of Jesus, 'Isa' (Jesus) being his first name. However, this is not the case. 'Mesih' or 'Messiah' is a title, not a name. The English word 'Christ' comes from the Greek, whereas 'Messiah' is a Hebrew word. Both words mean the same: 'the annointed One'. But what does calling Jesus 'the anointed One' mean?

First, we may note that Jesus made very few claims himself to be the Messiah. It was not a title that he used when talking about himself. One reason for this was probably the many different ideas about the 'Messiah' that were going around in first-century Palestine. It was a title that could very easily be misunderstood.

We obtain important information about Jesus as Messiah from the events surrounding his birth. As the disciples followed Jesus, they would surely have grown to know and love his mother Mary and his brothers and sisters. As they learnt more about Jesus, Mary would probably have shared with them the details of how Jesus was born that we looked at in chapter one.

One of the stories she must have told the disciples was of how there were shepherds looking after their flocks near Bethlehem on the night that Jesus was born.[31] Suddenly an angel of the Lord appeared to them and they were terrified. The angel said, 'Do not be afraid. I bring you good news of great joy that will be for all people. Today in the town of David a Saviour has been born to you; he is Messiah, the Lord.'

The crucial test of whether Jesus would be the true Messiah came at his baptism. This was followed immediately by his temptations for forty days in the desert. We have already seen, in chapter two, how that voice from heaven at the baptism of Jesus linked together two key truths about the Messiah that were both present in the Old Testament writings.

Most people at the time of Jesus saw the coming Messiah as mainly a political figure who would bring the Jews political salvation from their Roman oppressors. Indeed the word 'salvation' was seen by many as being mainly a political word, just as it is for many people today. Most people completely missed the emphasis in the Old Testament on the Messiah being the servant who would come to save people from their sin, not just from their political oppression.

In fact, the name 'Jesus' means 'Saviour'. It was no accident that Jesus received this name. When an angel appeared to Mary to tell her that she was going to give birth to a son, she was told, 'You are to give him the name Jesus, because he will save his people from their sins.'[32]

So in the idea of the coming Messiah was *both* the idea of a glorious king who would bring in a new age of peace *and* the idea of a suffering servant who, through his suffering, would save people from their sin. And in Jesus both of these ideas blend together. Jesus perfectly fulfilled that twofold vision that the heavenly voice had given him at his baptism. None of Satan's temptations had been able to deflect him from bringing in God's glorious kingdom through the way of being a suffering servant.

But Jesus demonstrated that he really was the Messiah, God's 'anointed One', for this special task, not so much by his claims in words, as by the demonstration of his life and of his love.

This is perhaps why, when people recognized Jesus as the Messiah, he often urged them to keep it to themselves. He knew very well what would happen if the message was spread that 'Jesus is the Messiah'. People would immediately get the wrong idea. They could even start a revolt or try to make him a political

'Messiah' by force. No, Jesus had to go right to the end of his life to demonstrate that he was indeed a 'suffering servant'. Only then would all the facts be available for everyone to see that he truly was the Messiah in all the fullest dimensions of Old Testament prophecy.

When Peter, one of Jesus' disciples, recognized clearly that Jesus was indeed 'the Messiah of God', Jesus strictly warned him not to tell this to anyone.[33] It is also significant that Jesus immediately began to talk of how he would have to suffer at the end of his life.[34] This connection of thought is no accident. Jesus underlines the fact that the Messiah was a suffering Messiah.

When demons in people started shouting out that Jesus was the Messiah, he refused to let them speak.[35] As the forces of darkness clashed with the authority of the kingdom of God, *they* had no doubt who Jesus really was!

It was only when Jesus was well away from the big cities and in the despised area of Samaria that he very clearly stated he was the Messiah. And he deliberately chose a person to tell who was an outcast in the eyes of the Jews — the Samaritan woman at the well whom we mentioned in chapter five.

After Jesus had told the woman that God was looking for people who would worship him in spirit and in truth, the woman said, 'I know that Messiah is coming. When he comes, he will explain everything to us.'

Jesus declared, 'I who speak to you am he.'[36]

A pause for thought

The minds of the disciples must have been in turmoil on many occasions as they listened to the claims of Jesus and watched what he did. A man who claimed to forgive sins, a man who had authority over nature, a man in whom they could detect no sin — the Son of Man, the Messiah . . . It soon became clear to them that God was revealing himself in Jesus in a special way, because Jesus was living out before them so much of what they knew about the character of God. It almost seemed as if God himself was drawing close to them in Jesus.

But what was the connection between Jesus and God? Before

we look further at some of the claims of Jesus, let us consider together a simple illustration.

Imagine that you are living in a world of only two dimensions. If you like, we can call this world 'Flat-land' because it has only length and width. You notice that in 'Flat-land' there are three large rings painted on the surface, separated from each other by a considerable distance. There is no apparent connection between the rings, except that they are of the same size.

One day a prophet comes in to Flat-land and proclaims to all the people: 'The three red rings are one!' Of course you would not believe him, and neither would anyone else. They take the prophet to each ring in turn and make him walk around it.

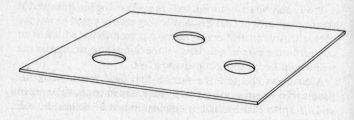

Any idiot could see that the three rings were quite separate. You could almost hear the people saying to the prophet 'You must be mad! What you are claiming is logically absurd! Even a small child can see that these three rings cannot be one.'

The people would be perfectly correct. In Flat-land there is no way that the three rings could be one.

But now imagine that an extra dimension is suddenly added to Flat-land. Not only is there length and breadth, but now there is height as well. The prophet returns triumphantly, carrying with him an enormous pipe, twisted into a curious three-dimensional shape. At first everyone thinks that the prophet is even madder than before! But as he steadily threads his giant pipe through the three red rings, some people at last understand what is going on.

With the extra dimension added to Flat-land, the impossible has become possible — the three rings have become one.

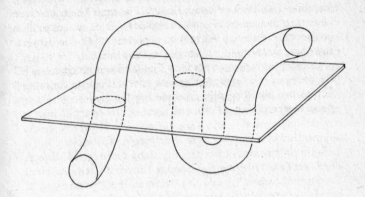

As the three-dimensional object touches two-dimensional space, so it will 'appear' three times in those two dimensions. Each one of these 'appearances' will be of the same essential object, each 'appearance' will have the same basic character, but to see these three as one as a Flat-lander is quite impossible. It is the extra dimension which makes all the difference.

When God reveals himself in our present world of limited dimensions, we must expect apparent paradoxes. God is not limited by any dimensions. He is a limitless being breaking into a very limited world of people whose brains operate within the scope of three dimensions plus time. If there are no paradoxes in revelations of God, then you should be suspicious. An absence of paradox suggests that somebody may have made the whole thing up, using data from their very limited three-dimensional sensory experiences.

I do not intend the above illustration to say anything to us about God himself. The whole purpose of the picture is to show us how we *cannot* understand God in the present world, not how we *can* comprehend him.

If you think that this all sounds very far from the comforting world of our everyday experience, then you should listen to physicists talking about their recent views concerning the structure of matter and the origins of the universe. Physicists sometimes talk about 'singularities' — events which are so unique and distinct from other events with which we are more familiar that they are beyond our present ability to either measure or understand. What happens if something (or somebody?) goes into a black hole? We do not know (though science fiction writers have great fun guessing). What happened during the first few micro-seconds after the Big Bang with which our present universe began? That is another 'singularity' that is beyond our present information boundaries. However, we do apparently know roughly what the situation was about a millisecond (10^{-3} second) after the Big Bang had started. Robert Boyd, professor of physics in London University, tells us that at the time there was a 'space with a temperature approaching 10^{14}K having already expanded to a volume 300 metres in diameter but containing all the mass/energy the Universe contains now'.[37]

I do not know about you, but when I look up at the stars on a clear night, I have quite a problem imagining all of *that* packed into an area not much bigger than a football pitch. But I am asked to believe, by very respectable physicists, that this was indeed the situation at the time when the universe was at a stage remotely distant from the present.

If this stretches your credulity, then you should read what some physicists are writing about current attempts to unify all the forces of the universe in one grand 'unified field theory'. Paul Davies, professor of theoretical physics at the University of Newcastle-upon-Tyne, talks about one 'conceivable scenario' for the creation of the universe:[38]

> In the beginning, 11-dimensional space time erupted spontaneously out of literally nothing . . . The shape of space need not initially have been specially ordered; it could have been chaotic and turbulent. In some regions, inevitably, the configuration would have been such that the competition of forces produced a huge repulsion. As a result, three space dimensions began to expand at an accelerating rate, while the remaining dimensions spontaneously

rolled themselves into a 7-sphere.

If you are a physicist, then I am sure that you have no problem grappling with concepts involving eleven dimensions, but for us lesser mortals, the ideas are mind-stretching, to say the least.

So, if our minds have to be stretched away beyond the common sense data of our daily experience in order to begin to understand the universe in which we live, how much more should a true revelation of God be expected to test our comprehension!

I hope you will keep the 'Flat-land' illustration in mind as we continue with the claims of Jesus. As we have already seen, there is no doubt that many of the claims of Jesus we have looked at make it look as if he was indeed claiming equality with God himself. But there are perhaps other interpretations that we could suggest — for example, that Jesus was only claiming that God's power was flowing through him in a new and special way.

In fact, at other times Jesus made some quite direct and extraordinary claims which make such an interpretation impossible. These claims resulted in the final confrontation with the Jewish authorities which led to his death.

For example, Jesus claimed that he had come from heaven to earth and that he had always existed. Once Jesus declared to the astonished crowds, 'I am the bread of life . . . I am the living bread that came down from heaven. If a man eats of this bread, he will live for ever.'[39]

So Jesus pointed to himself as the true source of heavenly life. At another time Jesus said, 'Before Abraham was born, I am!'[40]

We may wonder exactly what Jesus was claiming when he said this, but the people who listened to him had absolutely no doubt. We read that 'they picked up stones to stone him'. Why did they do that? Because it was a Jewish law that blasphemers against God should be stoned. The Old Testament states clearly that for the Jews, 'if anyone curses his God, he will be held responsible; anyone who blasphemes the name of the Lord must be put to death. The entire assembly must stone him.'[41]

So Jesus' Jewish listeners realized he was saying that he was eternally pre-existent, and immediately wanted to stone him for blasphemy.

When Jesus prayed to God his Father, he said, 'And now,

Father, glorify me in your presence with the glory I had with you *before the world began* . . . I want those you have given me to be with me where I am, and to see my glory, the glory you have given me because you loved me *before the creation of the world*.'[42]

Nothing could be clearer. Jesus is stating here that he had always existed.

There was another occasion when Jesus again pointed to himself as the source of eternal life. He said he was like a 'good shepherd' who 'lays down his life for the sheep'.[43]

Jesus continued, 'I give them eternal life, and they shall never perish; no one can snatch them out of my hand. My Father, who has given them to me, is greater than all; no one can snatch them out of my Father's hand. I and the Father are one.'[44] Again we read that the Jews picked up stones to stone Jesus. But Jesus said to them, 'I have shown you many great miracles from the Father. For which of these do you stone me?'

'We are not stoning you for any of these,' replied the Jews, 'but for blasphemy, because you, a mere man, claim to be God.'

It is vital to understand that the words of Jesus only have these extraordinary implications when placed firmly in the context of Jewish culture. If Jesus had been born a Hindu, then no one would have been the least surprised if Jesus had said, 'I and my Father are one', because in Hindu religious thought, God is the absolute ground of all being, and there is a sense, according to this philosophy, in which we all share a oneness with God. But the concept of God in the Jewish religion at the time of Jesus was totally different from such an idea, and that is precisely why his listeners interpreted his words as blasphemy. The only way we can correctly interpret the words of someone is according to their precise historical context.

That is why it was also so shocking when in another place Jesus said to Philip, one of his followers, 'Don't you know me, Philip, even after I have been among you such a long time? Anyone who has seen me has seen the Father. How can you say, "Show us the Father"? Don't you believe that I am in the Father, and that the Father is in me?'[45]

These claims are not the same as saying that God has a partner. He was claiming, rather, that he was of the same essence as God. He was claiming that there was a spiritual continuity between himself and God.

If you go to an ocean with a bucket and bring a bucketful of ocean water home with you, the water in the bucket is of the same essence as the water in the ocean. Indeed it *is* the ocean water. It has exactly the same constituents as the water in the ocean. It contains examples of all that you might find in the ocean. But it is not the ocean itself! The ocean is too vast to comprehend, but when we see a cross-section of it, we begin to understand.

Jesus was not claiming to be God in all his majesty and glory. The New Testament is perfectly clear that 'No man has seen God at any time'. Jesus himself prayed to his heavenly Father. We have already seen that he was a true human being.

So what happened when Jesus was born in Bethlehem? At that moment in time he left all the glory and wonder of heaven and took on a human form. He became human in order to show God's love to suffering mankind. He came with all the authority, power, holiness and love of God so that we might understand God more fully and come to know him for ourselves. Jesus was as much of God as you can fit into space, time and history. If he had come as God in all his glory, then we would have been blinded and consumed by his very presence!

In Jesus there is a real continuity with suffering mankind, but there is also a real continuity with God. Think about one of those three red rings. In Flat-land one ring is very much part of that particular two-dimensional world. It is so continuous with that world that a Flat-lander would find it difficult to understand that it could be continuous with anything outside that world. But with the superior view of three-dimensional people, we can easily see that it can indeed be continuous with the pipe curved through space. Yet it is not the whole pipe! It is not, if you like, the pipe in all its wholeness and fullness. The ring is a perfect expression of what the pipe is while it is touching a two-dimensional area.

Notice that one ring in this illustration is not simply an 'appearance' of the pipe, which may then 'appear' in a different way in another place.

Each ring is unique in its position on the three-dimensional pipe, and in this sense each one is different, even though each ring perfectly expresses the oneness and unity of the pipe.

Please notice again that I am not trying to 'prove' anything about the being of God by using this simple illustration. I am simply using it to try to clarify the data which we have in the life and teachings of Jesus of Nazareth. And I am certainly not asking you to believe immediately that all these claims are true! For the moment, I am concerned only that we understand the claims that Jesus actually made and that we do not jump to the wrong conclusions because of his use of certain expressions or phrases. Remember that Jesus was a monotheist right to the end of his life!

But I think you will have to agree that the data we find in the New Testament only makes sense when we understand that Jesus was claiming to be both completely human and completely divine. Otherwise, how could he forgive sins? How could he have power and authority over nature? How could he accept worship? How could he point so naturally to belief in *himself* rather than just a belief in his teaching?

For example, Jesus said, 'I am the way, and the truth, and the life. No one comes to the Father except through me.'[46] Do not forget that he used the expression 'Father' for 'God'.

At one of the big Jewish feasts, Jesus stood up in Jerusalem in the middle of a large crowd of people and proclaimed, 'If a man is thirsty, let him come to me and drink. Whoever believes in me, as the Scripture has said, streams of living water will flow from within him.'[47]

During that same week at the feast he said, 'If you knew me, you would know my Father also.'[48]

On another occasion Jesus said, 'I am the resurrection and the life. He who believes in me will live, even though he dies; and whoever lives and believes in me will never die.'[49]

Jesus also saw himself as the long-promised king that all the people had been waiting for — not as a political leader, but as the one who had all the kingly authority of God himself. When Jesus was being questioned by Pilate, the Roman governor of Palestine, following his arrest, he told him, 'You are right in saying I am a king. In fact for this reason I was born, and for this reason I came into the world, to testify to the truth. Everyone on the side of truth listens to me.'[50]

As we have already seen, Jesus pictured himself as the Son of

Man returning to earth with all the angels with him in order to judge the world. He then talked about *himself* as the king who will be sitting on his throne in heavenly glory with all the nations gathered before him![51]

So there is simply no way in which you can say that Jesus was just another religious teacher with an important ethical message for mankind. Nor can you believe that he was only a prophet. His claims are so extraordinary that he must have been mad if they are not indeed true. Frequently the New Testament tells us that his listeners in fact thought he was crazy. For example, after Jesus had talked about himself as being the Good Shepherd, many of the Jews said, 'He is demon-possessed and raving mad. Why listen to him?'[52] Even Jesus' own family thought that Jesus was out of his mind soon after he had started his public ministry![53]

Like those who originally listened to the claims of Jesus we have to decide one way or the other about Jesus. We cannot live with a comfortable idea that he was just another religious teacher and still keep our intellectual integrity. The data we possess does not allow it.

If Jesus was not indeed God clothing himself with our humanity in order to reveal himself to us in a new and special way, then he must at best have been mentally unbalanced, or at worst been a cunning deceiver. Where do you find people these days who claim equality with God? In mental hospitals!

But the strange fact is that, out of all the many varied people who have lived in this world and have claimed equality with God, Jesus is the only one who has ever been taken seriously. And, of all people, it was a group of monotheistic Jews who lived with Jesus for three years who were the first to put their trust in him . . .

Jesus as the Son of God

If you have read some parts of the New Testament, you will have noticed that it talks about Jesus as the 'Son of God' very frequently. You may also have noticed that I have deliberately avoided the phrase so far in this book, because I know how misunderstood it can be.

First we must understand that the term 'Son of God' has absolutely no physical meaning. Centuries ago there were some people who heard Christians using the phrase, and so thought that Christians believe God had actually had some physical relation with Mary and so had a son! This idea is of course blasphemous to any follower of Jesus and indeed to any true believer in God. 'God is spirit', said Jesus, and there can be no physical relationship between God and man. God is eternal and has neither beginning nor end. Of course God can never physically have a son!

You will notice that Jesus claimed to be pre-existent in heaven for all eternity before coming into the world. So his human body was physically born, but Jesus himself was eternal. At that moment in time in Bethlehem, the eternal Jesus took on a human body in order to be a servant to suffering mankind. Though he had always existed before that moment, it was part of God's great loving plan that he should exist among us in a different form for that short space of thirty-three years.

What did the phrase 'Son of God' mean for the Jewish people who listened to Jesus? It is clear that they were not shocked by the phrase as if they thought it meant that God had produced a son. In fact, the phrase 'Son of God' was rather familiar to both the Greeks and the Jews of the Roman Empire. For the Greek world it was a phrase commonly used to refer to some popular hero, and the Jews were familiar with the term because it was used in the Old Testament for the kings of Israel. Many of the Psalms refer to the king as 'God's Son', and with time the Jews came to see these references as referring also to the coming Messiah.

When the Jews talked about King David as 'God's Son', they certainly did not mean that there was any physical relationship between God and King David. 'Son of' was a common Hebrew expression meaning 'having the same character as'. When used of an earthly king, it therefore meant that he shared something of God's kingly authority and power.

The Hebrew for the English phrase 'human beings' is 'sons of men'. In the Old Testament bad people are often called 'sons of wickedness' — that is, they are completely wicked, or share completely in the character of wickedness.

We must not confuse the model with the reality. We all know what a physical father–son relationship *should* be like — it should express love and mutal respect. The son should express the desires and character of the father. The father should love his son and rejoice to see his life expressed through him.

In many different languages the phrase 'son of the road' is used to refer to a 'traveller'. Obviously it does not mean that they were born from the road! It is vivid analogy and no one would be stupid enough to think it had a physical meaning.

So Jesus took a vivid model which was in common use at the time, and used it to express the very special relationship that he had with his heavenly Father. He took the phrase 'Son of God' and gave it a particular meaning as he applied it to himself.

There is no doubt that one of the meanings of the phrase is linked with the claim of Jesus to be the Messiah. As we saw earlier, as soon as Jesus was baptized, the voice from heaven said, 'This is my *Son* whom I love . . .'[54]

And it was right after this that Jesus faced Satan's temptations in the wilderness. Again and again Satan said, '*If* you are the Son of God . . .'[55] But Jesus refused to be deflected from his true Messianic role as a suffering servant.

When the Jewish high priest was questioning Jesus following his arrest, he said, 'Tell us if you are Christ (Messiah), the Son of God.'

'Yes, it is as you say', Jesus replied. 'But I say to all of you: In future you will see the Son of Man sitting at the right hand of the Mighty One and coming on the clouds of heaven.'[56]

Then the high priest tore his clothes and said, 'He has spoken blasphemy! Why do we need any more witnesses?'

You see how, for the high priest, the term 'Messiah' naturally went together with the expression 'Son of God'?

But Jesus did not only use the phrase 'Son of God' about himself as an alternative way of claiming to be the Messiah. He also talked in a very personal way about his heavenly Father. For the disciples God was '*our* Father'.[57] But for Jesus he was always '*my* Father'.

'All things have been committed to me by my Father. No one knows the Son except the Father, and no one knows the

Father except the Son and those to whom the Son chooses to
reveal him.'[58]

It is quite clear that Jesus was not claiming to be a popular Greek
hero at this point! He was saying that he had a very special
relationship with his Father.

After Jesus had healed someone on the Sabbath, he said to the
Jews who opposed him, 'My Father is always at his work to this
very day, and I, too, am working.'[59]

Then we read that 'for this reason the Jews tried all the harder
to kill him; not only was he breaking the Sabbath, but he was
even calling God his own Father, making himself equal with
God.'

Jesus continued, 'Just as the Father raises the dead and gives
them life, even so the Son gives life to whom he is pleased to give
it . . . whoever hears my word and believes him who sent me has
eternal life and will not be condemned; he has crossed over from
death to life . . . A time is coming and has now come when the
dead will hear the voice of the Son of God and those who hear
will live . . .'[60]

Jesus claimed a perfect relationship with his heavenly Father.
What the Father did, he did. He said that he was the only one who
really knew the Father. If anyone wanted to know what the
Father was like, then they should look at him.

If Jesus was like a red ring in relation to the whole pipe, is it so
strange to think that he could have expressed perfectly as much of
the nature of the pipe as could be expressed in two dimensions? Is
it so odd that one red ring should be of the same oneness as the
whole pipe and yet also have a relationship with another ring
elsewhere in the pipe?

Why are the claims of Jesus important?

Illustrations may have helped to make the claims of Jesus clearer.
But you may still be wondering why they are so important.

If God wanted to send mankind some new teachings about his
love and holiness, about sin, and about God's concern for social
justice, then surely sending a prophet would be quite sufficient?

Why was there any need for God to appear among human beings in this extraordinary way? Surely there could have been other ways for God to communicate his character to our limited minds? Why did he come at all?

1   Mark 1:23—28
2   John 2:11
3   John 6:2
4   John 9:33
5   Luke 18:43
6   Luke 11:14—20
7   Luke 7:11—17
8   John 6:14
9   Deuteronomy 18:15—22
10 Matthew 21:10
11 John 4:44
12 Luke 13:33
13 Luke 5:17—26
14 Luke 7:36—50
15 Matthew 8:23—27
16 Matthew 14:22—33
17 Matthew 14:13—21, Matthew 15:29—39
18 John 8:46
19 Matthew 4:18—20
20 1 Peter 2:22
21 Hebrews 4:15
22 Matthew 5:17
23 Matthew 8:20
24 Matthew 11:16—19
25 Matthew 20:20—28
26 John 13:1—17
27 Luke 5:24
28 Matthew 24:30
29 Daniel 7:13—14
30 Matthew 26:64
31 Luke 2:8—14
32 Matthew 1:21
33 Luke 9:20—21
34 Luke 9:22

35 Luke 4:41
36 John 4:25–26
37 *Faith and Thought* Volume 109, no. 2, pp. 111–26, 1982
38 *New Scientist*, 9 February 1984, pp. 31–33
39 John 6:48, 51
40 John 8:58–59
41 Leviticus 24:15–16
42 John 17:5, 24
43 John 10:11
44 John 10:28–33
45 John 14:9–10
46 John 14:6
47 John 7:37–38
48 John 8:19
49 John 11:25
50 John 18:37
51 Matthew 25:31–34
52 John 10:20
53 Mark 3:21
54 Matthew 3:17
55 Matthew 4:3, 6
56 Matthew 26:63–64
57 Matthew 6:9
58 Matthew 11:27
59 John 5:16–18
60 John 5:21, 24–25

9

The Death and Resurrection of Jesus

Some people think that because Christians talk about the death of Jesus, this means that they believe that God somehow forsook his 'chosen one', or that something happened to Jesus apparently against God's will. Is this really what they believe?

I am deliberately talking in this chapter about the death and resurrection of Jesus in one breath, as it were, so that we keep the meaning of these two events firmly connected in our minds. Both the death and resurrection of Jesus were in any case so close to each other in time (within three days) that it comes quite naturally to consider them together.

Unfortunately, the cross as a symbol has been used and misused by so many nominal Christians down the centuries that its original historical meaning has been completely lost. When the barbaric Crusaders came to invade the Middle East, they came with bright red crosses painted on their shields and wielding swords in their hands. Any thinking follower of Jesus must feel ashamed as he remembers those armies. Of course the common people did not have the New Testament in their own language in those days, otherwise history might have turned out differently. How surprised they would have been to read the actual teachings of Jesus and see what he said about war and violence! When just *one* of his followers (Peter) lifted his sword to defend Jesus at the time of his arrest, Jesus told him to put his sword away. Spiritual battles cannot be fought with physical weapons.

The Crusaders and their political leaders believed that Christianity is about defending pieces of land, about holy sites. But in fact the kingdom of God is not about geography, about places, at all.

Sadly today, even at a time when the New Testament is translated into many languages, there are still those calling themselves Christians who use violence to further their ends. Some even think that they can defend the teachings of Jesus with weapons. Not two kilometres from where I am sitting there are men with gold crosses hanging around their necks as they casually snipe at people with their automatic weapons. What they are doing is totally opposite to the way that Jesus taught.

So one can quite understand if the cross has negative associations for some people for historical or political reasons. In fact, for many living in so called 'Christian' countries, it has become an almost meaningless symbol. You see crosses on top of churches, in village squares, in little boxes by the roadside, round people's necks — but if you asked people what the cross *meant*, they would probably have only the vaguest idea or none. It has become superstition, or a lucky charm, or just a bit of decoration.

Let us go back to the life of Jesus himself. Let us try to put aside as far as we are able the negative feelings that we have about the cross as a symbol, and let us try to see what actually happened to Jesus at the end of his public ministry. Could it really be that God would allow his chosen one to experience such a cruel torture? Before we examine this crucial question, we also need to ask whether Jesus really *did* die on a cross. For if he never really died, then there is nothing that needs explaining . . .

Did Jesus die on a cross?

Down the centuries there have been various people who have denied that Jesus of Nazareth ever died in Palestine. For example, some have claimed that Jesus did not really die on the cross, but only swooned. There are others who believe that someone else was crucified in the place of Jesus, and that Jesus himself was caught up to heaven without dying. There are even those who believe that Jesus died a normal death in some other country right outside Palestine!

As a scientist I like to start on the side of the sceptics and take a hard look at the evidence. First we are going to look at the historical evidence for the death of Jesus that we have from people who did *not* believe Jesus was the Messiah. If we look only at evidence from the New Testament, it may be that the writers were biased or made up some of what they wrote. In fact the New Testament documents are just as historically verifiable as any other. But when the evidence comes from people who did *not* believe in Jesus, then it may seem more disinterested and convincing.

We may briefly list some of the evidence as follows:

The letter of Mara bar Serapion Sometime after AD 73 a Syrian called Mara bar Serapion, who was in prison at the time, sent a letter to his son Serapion. The letter is today in the British Museum in London. He wrote the letter to encourage his son in the pursuit of wisdom, so he pointed out to his son that those who persecuted wise men often themselves face troubles of their own later on. As examples, he gave the deaths of Socrates, Pythagoras and Jesus:

> 'What advantage did the Athenians gain from putting Socrates to death? Famine and plague were upon them as judgment for their crime. What advantage did the men of Samos gain from burning Pythagoras? In a moment their land was covered with sand. What advantage did the Jews gain from executing their wise king? It was just after that that their kingdom was abolished. God justly avenged these three wise men: the Athenians died of hunger; the Samians were overwhelmed by the sea; the Jews, ruined and driven from their land, live in complete dispersion.'

This letter is especially interesting because of its early date and because bar Serapion clearly had no particular interest in presenting evidence for the death of Jesus. It was simply an accepted fact at the time he was writing. Everyone knew that Jesus had died. It would be like someone writing today and mentioning in passing the assassination of President Kennedy. We do not need to comment further on such well-known historical facts.

Josephus was a Jewish historian who was born in AD 37. At various times he belonged to different Jewish religious sects, but ended up by becoming a Pharisee — as we have seen, hardly the group of Jews who appreciated Jesus most!

When the Jewish revolt against Rome broke out in AD 66, Josephus was appointed commander of the rebels in Galilee and played an important role in resisting the Roman army. However, after resistance in Galilee was crushed in the summer of AD 67, he was put in prison. Eventually obtaining his release, he devoted the second part of his life to writing a history of the Jewish people. In the course of this history there are several references to Jesus, as well as some details about other people mentioned in the New Testament, such as John the Baptist.

Josephus was never a follower of Jesus. So the following passage, quoted from his *Antiquities* volume 18, written in the early part of the second century, is of special interest. The quote here is from the Arabic version which is contained in 'Kitab Al-Unwan Al-Mukallal Bi-Fadail Al-Hikma Al-Mutawwaj Bi-Anwa Al-Falsafa Al-Manduh Bi-Haqaq Al-Marifa':

> At this time there was a wise man who was called Jesus. And his conduct was good, and he was known to be virtuous. And many people from among the Jews and the other nations became his disciples. *Pilate condemned him to be crucified and to die.* And those who had become his disciples did not abandon his discipleship. They reported that he had appeared to them three days after his crucifixion and that he was alive; accordingly, he was perhaps the Messiah concerning whom the prophets have recounted wonders.

Cornelius Tacitus was a Roman historian and governor of Asia in the early part of the second century. In AD 112 he wrote about the reign of the Roman Emperor Nero, and refers in passing to the death of Jesus. At the time of Nero a large fire destroyed much of Rome, and there was apparently a rumour that Nero himself had ordered the fire to be started. Tacitus wrote:

> To suppress the rumour, Nero falsely charged with guilt and punished with most exquisite tortures, the persons commonly called Christians, who were hated for their enormities. *Christus, the founder of the name, was put to death* by Pontius Pilate, procurator of Judea in the reign of Tiberius; but the pernicious superstition, repressed for a time, broke out again, not only through Judea, where the mischief originated, but through the city of Rome also.

It is clear from the quote that Tacitus had no time for the teachings of Jesus. On the contrary he called them a 'pernicious superstition'! Yet he knew it was a historical fact that Jesus had been put to death — just as everybody else knew.

Thallus was a historian born in Samaria in AD 52. However, his writings have disappeared, and we only know of them from fragments quoted by other writers. For example Julius Africanus, writing at about AD 221, discussed the darkness which occurred at the time that Jesus died:

> Thallus, in the third book of his histories, explains this darkness as an eclipse of the sun — unreasonably, as it seems to me.

An eclipse of the sun was clearly unreasonable because it did not take place at the time of the full moon, and it was the time of the full moon when Jesus died. But the important point here is that not only the *fact* of the death of Jesus, but also the details concerning the event which took place at his death, were well known to Thallus, as a non-Christian Samaritan historian writing in the first century.

Lucian was a second-century satirical writer who attacked Jesus and his followers. Yet he referred to Jesus as:

> The man who was crucified in Palestine because he introduced this new cult into the world . . . Furthermore, their first lawgiver persuaded them that they were all brothers one of another after they had sinned once for all by denying the Greek gods and by worshipping that crucified sophist himself and living under his laws.

Even the most bitter opponents of Jesus realized that he had been crucified in Palestine!

Rabbinical literature. After the fall of Jerusalem in AD 70, the Jews established a new centre for their religion in western Palestine. For the next 130 years a succession of rabbis (Jewish leaders) wrote down the Jewish laws and traditions in a collection of writings which came to be known as the *Mishnah*. The

Mishnah became an object of study both in Palestine and Babylon, and various commentaries were written about it. The commentaries were called the *Gemaras*, and the *Mishnah* plus the *Gemaras* together are generally called the *Talmud*.

The *Talmud* contains some of the Jewish traditions about Jesus. These are important for our historical purpose here, because these traditions are generally very hostile to Jesus. They reflect the general rejection of Jesus by the Jewish leaders that we have already noted.

There is one particularly interesting passage in the section in the *Talmud* known as the 'Sanhedrin', which comes from the period AD 78 to 200:

> Jesus was hanged on Passover eve. Forty days previously the herald had cried, 'He is being led out for sin, because he has practised sorcery and led Israel astray and enticed them into apostasy. Whoever has anything to say in his defence, let him come and declare it.' As nothing was brought forward in his defence, he was hanged on Passover eve.

Hanging in various forms was traditionally permitted by Jewish law, and the term also included hanging by crucifixion.

Together with the historical evidence for writers who did not believe in Jesus, we also have the writings of the New Testament itself. It is a remarkable fact that more than one third of each of the four accounts of Jesus concerns the events surrounding his death. Again we see how these accounts are not normal biographies. What modern biographer would spend more than one third of his book writing about a person's death? But Matthew, Mark, Luke and John are deliberately focusing on the most crucial reason why Jesus came into this world. If you miss this, you miss everything.

How did Jesus die?

What were the key events which lead up to the death of Jesus?

Jesus frequently predicted to his disciples that he was going to die and then rise again from the dead. For example, after Peter had recognized that Jesus was indeed the Messiah, 'Jesus strictly warned them not to tell this to anyone. And he said, "The Son of Man must suffer many things and be rejected by the elders, chief priests and teachers of the law, and he must be killed and on the third day be raised to life." '[1]

When Peter told Jesus that this would never happen to him, Jesus spoke to him in the strongest language, 'Out of my sight, Satan! You are a stumbling block to me; you do not have in mind the things of God, but the things of men.'[2]

Peter surely never forgot those words. He wanted Jesus to be a glorious Messiah, a reigning king — but what was all this about suffering? Jesus told Peter bluntly that he did not understand the plan of God. The Son of Man *must* suffer . . .

All his life Jesus had this deep sense of destiny, that he was heading towards a climax which would fulfil his purpose in coming into the world. So we read that 'As the time approached for him to be taken up to heaven, Jesus resolutely set out for Jerusalem.'[3]

Jesus knew that he was going to die in Jerusalem. In one of the villages on the way, some Pharisees came to Jesus and said to him, 'Leave this place and go somewhere else. Herod wants to kill you.'[4]

Jesus told them that anyway he would be continuing his journey '. . . for surely no prophet can die outside Jerusalem!'[5]

Jesus was timing his arrival in Jerusalem very carefully with the Jewish Passover feast. He knew precisely what was going to happen to him there. But still he kept on. The meaning of the Passover feast held a crucial clue to the meaning of his death.

As Jesus and his disciples finally approached Jerusalem at the start of the week of the Passover feast, a great crowd came out to meet him. They placed their coats and the branches of trees across the road before him as a sign of respect, and shouted out 'Praise be to the Son of David!'[6] The whole city was stirred up, wondering who Jesus was.

The next few days were packed with teaching as Jesus used every moment to challenge the crowds who had come for the feast, and to explain many important points to his disciples. Much of his teaching at the time was about events of the future.[7]

During the week, Jesus celebrated the Passover feast with his disciples. This was a way of remembering how God had provided a way of sacrifice in order to save the first-born of the Jewish families when they were in Egypt. An angel of death had passed over the country to judge the idols of the land and all those who were opposing God.[8] To escape the judgment of this angel of death, the Jewish people had been instructed to kill a sacrificial lamb and to place some of its blood on the doors of the house. Whenever the angel of death saw the blood, it would 'pass over' the household.

In this vivid symbolism is one of the main ideas about sacrifice that we find in the Old Testament — that the judgment of God could be prevented through sacrificial blood. Of course there was nothing magic in the blood itself. It was rather that the blood represented the death of an innocent animal in the place of the death of a sinful person. Certainly sacrificing an animal was an act of obedience to God. But it had a meaning far deeper than that. Death, or separation from God, was an inevitable consequence of sin. The person carrying out the sacrifice recognized that there was nothing *he* could do to remove his own sin. If fellowship with God was to be restored, the sin had to be paid for in death. It could be removed only through the sacrificial death of another.

Animal sacrifice was a vivid visual aid. It was not the real thing. Throughout the Old Testament we see that the symbol of animal sacrifice was pointing forward to an ultimate sacrifice for sin which was yet to come. Remember how John the Baptist pointed at Jesus and said, 'Look, the Lamb of God, who takes away the sin of the world!'[9]

As he ate the Passover meal with his disciples, Jesus took bread, gave thanks and broke it. As he gave it to his disciples he said, 'Take and eat; this is my body.'

Jesus then took a cup of the 'fruit of the vine' and said to them, 'Drink from it, all of you. This is my blood of the covenant, which is poured out for many for the forgiveness of sins.'[10]

The word 'covenant' here means a binding 'agreement'. As Jesus was about to be literally sacrificed on the cross, so his blood was given to seal an agreement or promise between God and man. He explained very clearly that his death was to be 'for many for the forgiveness of sins'. The bread was symbolizing his own body which was about to be 'broken' or given up for others during his intense torture on the cross.

Bread was then, as it is now, a basic ingredient of most diets of the world, and therefore a symbol of life. The 'fruit of the vine' was a symbol of blood. Ever since the death and resurrection of Jesus, his followers have remembered his death by eating bread and drinking the fruit of the vine together in a simple meal. In fact this remembrance meal itself is one of the main historical evidences for the death and resurrection of Jesus, because in the very earliest records we read of it happening among the followers of Jesus.

All over the world today you will find followers of Jesus meeting to remember his death and resurrection in this way. The meeting-place is not important. It may be in a simple room, or in a church, or outside in the open air. The meal is often called the 'Lord's Supper', emphasizing its historical origins, or 'Holy Communion', to underline the closeness that believers sense to God and to each other as they remember the death and resurrection of Jesus together. Jesus had died to take away their sins. Just as they share the bread and wine, so they share in Jesus' death. Their sins have been forgiven. They can share the communion, the fellowship, of newness of life with God.

On the very same evening of celebrating the Passover meal with his disciples, Jesus was arrested. This happened while he was praying on the Mount of Olives just across the Kidron Valley from the Dome of the Rock in present-day Jerusalem. One can still see today a grove of ancient olive trees — probably the place where Jesus was praying at the time.

Jesus was betrayed by one of his disciples called Judas for thirty silver coins. It was Judas who came with the Jewish leaders in order to arrest him. There was no doubt that they arrested the right man, because Judas himself came up and kissed Jesus in greeting so that the Jews would know who to arrest. Later on Judas was full of remorse for doing such a terrible thing and committed suicide.[11]

Following his arrest, Jesus was interrogated by Caiphas, the Jewish high priest, together with a council of Jewish leaders. Many false witnesses were brought before the council to give evidence against Jesus, but he refused to defend himself, remaining quite silent as they threw their false claims at him.[12] It was only when they asked him directly: 'Are you the Son of God?' that Jesus gave them the direct reply that they were waiting for: 'You are right in saying I am.'

Then his listeners said, 'Why do we need any more testimony? We have heard it from his own lips.'

It was because Jesus claimed so openly to be the Son of God that he was then taken to Pilate, who was the Roman governor of Palestine at the time, and had the final authority over matters of security in the area. When Jesus had been before the Jewish council, false witnesses had accused him of crimes 'against the temple' which would be likely to offend Jews.[14] But as he stood before the Roman governor, the false witnesses accused him of all kinds of things that would be most likely to upset Rome![15] They told Pilate that Jesus was a rival king to Caesar, that he opposed the paying of taxes to the emperor, and that he had started a revolt in Galilee which had spread all the way to Jerusalem!

But it was clear that Pilate did not feel threatened by these wild accusations. The fact that he felt no threat was good evidence that Jesus was *not* engaged in political activities. If Jesus had actually been leading a rebellion against Rome, the reaction of Pilate would have been very different.

As it was, Pilate obviously felt very relieved to hear that Jesus came from Galilee. That gave him a good excuse to send Jesus off to Herod, who was the Jewish tetrarch or 'local ruler' of the Galilee area. This was not the same Herod as the king who had been in power when Jesus was born. When that Herod had died, he had divided Palestine up into four areas which were then ruled by four of his sons. One of these was the Herod in front of whom Jesus was now brought.

At first Herod was pleased to see Jesus, because he thought Jesus might do a miracle for him.[16] Of course Jesus refused. As Herod asked more questions and the Jewish leaders threw more accusations, Jesus again refused to answer, remaining absolutely silent. So Herod and his soldiers took the easy way out. They dressed Jesus up like a king in an elegant robe, ridiculed and mocked him, and then sent him back to Pilate to make the final decision.

Pilate still sensed that Jesus was innocent and looked for a good excuse to have him released. It was the governor's custom at the time of the Passover feast to release a prisoner chosen by the crowd. There was a notorious criminal being held in prison at that time. His name was Barabbas, and he had been arrested for leading an armed rebellion. Pilate shouted out to the crowd, 'Which one do you want me to release to you: Barabbas, or Jesus who is called Christ (Messiah)?'[17]

The crowd all yelled out 'Barabbas!' and shouted at Pilate to crucify Jesus.

Finally Pilate was persuaded. He took a bowl of water and washed his hands in front of the crowd, 'I am innocent of this man's blood', he said. 'It is your responsibility.'[18]

The crowd replied, 'Let his blood be on us and on our children!'

Then Pilate released Barabbas. But he had Jesus flogged and then given to the Roman soldiers to be crucified. Pilate had no desire to stir up unnecessary trouble with the Jews. So Barabbas the revolutionary went free, and Jesus was crucified in his place.

The Roman soldiers had great fun with Jesus.[19] They stripped him and put a scarlet robe on him. Then they made a crown out of thorns and put it on his head. Placing a stick in the right hand of Jesus they knelt in front of him and mocked him saying, 'Hail, King of the Jews!'

They spat on Jesus and hit him repeatedly, but he did not resist, literally 'turning the other cheek' as he had taught his disciples to do in the Sermon on the Mount. After that he was led out to be crucified.

As we have already noted, crucifixion processions were a common sight in first-century Palestine. A condemned man would be forced to carry the 'patibulum', a heavy cross-beam which would be fixed to an upright tree or log of wood to make a cross. But by this time Jesus was so exhausted that he could not carry his own patibulum the whole way. The Roman soldiers picked out a North African in the crowd called Simon, and forced him to carry the patibulum for Jesus.[20]

The cross was not just an instrument of execution — it was also a means of torture. Crucifixion was a long, slow, lingering death.

Nails were hammered through the wrists or hands into the wood of the cross-beam. The prisoner was then raised up on the patibulum so that the full weight of his body dragged down on the nails tearing through the flesh. Under the feet there was a large ledge. By placing the feet on this ledge some of the weight of the body could be taken off the arms — but this only lengthened the process of dying.

The Roman soldiers took Jesus with two robbers to a place outside the city walls called 'Golgotha', which means 'The Place of the Skull'. The soldiers offered him a mild drug to relieve the pain.[21] But Jesus refused to take it. He refused to do anything to lessen the terrible reality of what he was going through.

As Jesus was lifted up in agony on the cross, he prayed for his tormentors, 'Father, forgive them, for they do not know what they are doing.'

What kind of love was this, that the one being tortured actually prayed that God would forgive his tormentors!

Meanwhile the Jewish rulers came to mock Jesus, even while he was hanging on the cross. They said, 'He saved others; let him save himself if he is the Christ (Messiah) of God, the Chosen One.'[22]

What a temptation it must have been for Jesus to call down all of God's power to deliver himself from the torture of death on the cross! Of course Jesus could have done that. At any moment he had the power to be called up to heaven, but he deliberately chose not to use that power. It was not God's will. His was the power of true submission. There was a great and amazing plan which could only be fulfilled through his death. Even his own disciples did not really understand what that plan involved. But Jesus knew that he had to drink death's last bitter drop.

Just as he had defeated all Satan's demands in the desert so that he could remain the true Messiah, the Suffering Servant, so now his mockers were putting before him basically the same temptation. Show your supernatural powers, Jesus! Come down off that shameful cross!

'Let God rescue him now if he wants him, for he said "I am the Son of God." '[23]

But if Jesus had done that, then his whole reason for coming into the world would have been destroyed. His love for us drove him right to the end.

And let us be in no doubt that it was Jesus himself who was dying there on that cross. There is absolutely no evidence that anyone else could have been crucified in his place. Both his mother and his mother's sister were standing there at the foot of the cross.[24] Would a mother not know her own son?

At the same time some of his disciples were watching him — people who had lived and worked with Jesus for three years.[25] They could not have been deceived about who was hanging there on the cross.

Then there were tough Roman soldiers keeping guard, and there was a whole crowd of people waiting near the cross, including many Jewish leaders. *They* knew Jesus well enough! How often they had been challenged and frustrated by his teaching as he stood up preaching before them in the public places in Jerusalem.

And on either side of Jesus were crucified two thieves. *They* also knew very well who Jesus was. In fact one of them started hurling insults at Jesus: 'Aren't you the Christ (Messiah)? Save yourself and us!'

But the other thief called on Jesus to save him, 'Jesus, remember me when you come into your kingdom.'

Jesus answered him, 'I tell you the truth, today you will be with me in paradise.'[26]

So the thief was able to enter God's kingdom at the eleventh hour of his life — simply by putting his trust in Jesus. But how could that be? The thief had no opportunity to work for his salvation. He was about to die. He had obviously not lived a good life. How could he go to paradise?

From twelve noon until three in the afternoon a strange darkness came over the land as Jesus still hung on the cross. Finally he cried out, 'It is finished!'[27]

Then Jesus died. When you read the sentence in English you may think that it is a cry of despair. But the original Greek means something different. It means 'It is completed.' The task of Jesus on earth had finished. So it was with a great cry of triumph that Jesus died.

As he died something extraordinary happened in the Jewish temple inside the city. There was a great curtain separating the holiest place in the temple from the rest of the building where people worshipped. The priests could go inside the holiest of areas only once a year during a time of special sacrifice. No one else was allowed in at any time on pain of death. As Jesus died, the heavy curtain was split in two from top to bottom.[28] No longer was there a barrier separating sinful man from a holy God. Through the death of Jesus that barrier was destroyed.

It was now Friday afternoon, sometime after 3 p.m. The Jewish Sabbath began officially at 6 p.m., and after that time the Jews were not allowed to do any work. So the Jewish leaders asked Pilate if he would have the legs broken of the three being crucified so that they would die quickly. In this way the bodies could be taken down before the Sabbath began.[29] Once the legs were broken, the person being crucified could no longer support his weight by resting his feet on the ledge. Death would come quickly.

Soldiers broke the legs of the two thieves, but when they came to Jesus, they saw that he was already dead.[30] Remember that these were Roman soldiers for whom crucifying people was routine. They knew a dead man when they saw him. But to make doubly sure, one of them pierced Jesus' side with his spear. An eyewitness, probably John himself, records how he saw a 'sudden flow of blood and water' coming from the wound.[30] That historical detail is important. It means that Jesus really had died. During the incredible stress of those hours on the cross, fluid had begun to collect around the heart of Jesus. Most probably the spear pierced the cardiac cavity itself, and the fluid came out with the blood. This was of course written before the days of modern medicine. The observer simply wrote down what he saw, without understanding its medical significance.

Today we understand the medical significance. It means that Jesus really was dead.

It was Joseph, a member of the Jewish council, who took the body of Jesus down from the cross.[31] Helped by Nicodemus, another secret sympathizer of Jesus who was also a member of the council,[32] Joseph wrapped the body of Jesus in long strips of burial linen, placing up to 34 kilograms of preservatives between the strips. It was probably only such important Jewish leaders who were allowed to come near the body, for fear of theft.

Joseph himself owned a new unused tomb which was in the garden close to the site of the crucifixion.[33] He and Nicodemus placed the body of Jesus in this tomb, which was carved out of the solid rock. Across the front of the tomb they rolled a great circular stone which ran in a trench especially cut for the purpose. All over the Middle East you can see examples of this type of tomb which date from Roman times (there are some good examples just outside Gaziantep in Turkey, for instance, as well as in Jerusalem itself). Once the circular stone had been pushed in front of the entrance to the tomb the trench was filled with earth and rocks to 'seal' the circular stone in place.

The Jewish leaders knew very well that Jesus had earlier claimed he was going to die and then rise again after three days.[34] To prevent any of Jesus' disciples stealing the body and then claiming that he had risen from the dead, they asked Pilate to put a guard on the tomb. Pilate agreed, and so the body of Jesus lay inside the solid rock, bound tightly by kilos of cloth and spices, with a massive stone in front of the tomb guarded by Roman soldiers.

Why did Jesus die?

I have spent some time explaining *how* Jesus died for the simple reason that the New Testament focuses so much on these historical events. But even if you believe that this is how Jesus died, this information will have little significance to you unless you also know *why* he died:

Jesus died for blasphemy The immediate legal reason why Jesus died was because he claimed equality with God. In the eyes of the Jews this was blasphemy, and in the eyes of the Roman authorities it was simply ridiculous.

We have already seen in chapter four that the Jewish authorities were looking for ways to kill Jesus from the very start of his public ministry. There were many reasons why they wanted him eliminated. His teaching was undermining their own authority.

With the masses he was immensely popular. He performed miracles that they could not do, so there was a considerable element of jealousy. And his emphasis on love and justice was irritating to a class of people who were concerned only with the outward keeping of religious regulations. His direct claims of equality with God were the final straw that broke the camel's back! The penalty for such blasphemy was obviously death.

After the arrest of Jesus, Caiphas the high priest accused him of blasphemy.[35] When Jesus was standing before Pilate, the Jews insisted, 'We have a law, and according to that law he must die, because he claimed to be the Son of God.'[36]

Legally Jesus was a condemned man from the very beginning of his public ministry. It was only his popularity with the people that had inhibited the Jews from having him arrested earlier.

In fact the death of Jesus by crucifixion is the final proof that he really was claiming equality with God. Without those claims the Jews would have had no legal basis for having him brought before the Roman governor — the only man who could order his death.

Jesus died as an example Jesus has always been the supreme example of how to accept suffering from the hands of others. He was sinless and totally innocent of any real crime. He never hit back at those that tormented him. His trial and subsequent death were completely unjust, but he never called on his heavenly Father to destroy the Jewish leaders or burn up the Roman authorities with fire.

As we have already seen, Jesus even prayed for those who were crucifying him as he hung on the cross asking his Father to forgive them.

All down the centuries there have been martyrs and men of faith who have looked to Jesus as their example in suffering. There have been those revolutionaries for just causes who have followed the way of passive resistance and by so doing have won the freedom of communities and nations. Many of them have died for what they believed in, literally following in the footsteps of Jesus by accepting death rather than giving up their beliefs.

The suffering of Jesus obviously made a deep impact on Peter, the disciple of Jesus who had denied him shortly after his arrest, and who had then felt bitterly sorry for what he had done.[37] Later Peter wrote to some followers of Jesus, 'Christ suffered for you, leaving you an example, that you should follow in his steps.'[38]

Accepting suffering as Jesus did is not a sign of weakness but a sign of power. Love is ultimately stronger than hate. It is the weak person, unable to control himself, who burns with anger, or who becomes consumed with a desire for revenge, or who is eaten up with jealousy. Such a person is a slave — a slave to his own passions. Jesus demonstrated true freedom by remaining totally unchained by all the evils which normally grip people's hearts. Immense power is released by that kind of freedom. But can we ever experience it for ourselves?

Jesus died as a sacrifice for sin If we think Jesus died only for the immediate legal reason of blasphemy, and as a wonderful example of suffering, then we have still missed the main point of why he came into the world. The main reason Jesus came into the world was to die as a sacrifice for sin.

This is not some special interpretation placed on his crucifixion by his disciples after his death. It was the basic understanding in the mind of Jesus from the very beginning. The true Messiah could not be a reigning king — a Son of Man coming on the clouds of heaven — without first being a suffering servant.

Many of the Old Testament prophecies in fact speak of the future suffering of the Messiah, particularly the book of the prophet Isaiah, written about 800 BC. A copy of this famous prophecy was found among the Dead Sea Scrolls. This particular copy dates from 100 years *before* the birth of Jesus, so we can be very sure that these words were not changed by the followers of Jesus later on. Here is what Isaiah said about the Messiah who was to come:

He was despised and rejected by men
a man of sorrows and familiar with suffering . . .

He was pierced for our transgressions,
he was crushed for our iniquities;
the punishment that brought us peace was upon him,
and by his wounds we are healed.

We all, like sheep, have gone astray,

each of us has turned to his own way;
and the Lord has laid on him the iniquity of us all.

He was oppressed and afflicted,
yet he did not open his mouth;
he was led like a lamb to the slaughter,
and as a sheep before her shearers is silent,
so he did not open his mouth . . .

He was assigned a grave with the wicked,
and with the rich in his death,
though he had done no violence,
nor was any deceit in his mouth . . .

He poured out his life unto death,
and was numbered with the transgressors.
For he bore the sin of many,
and made intercession for the transgressors.'[39]

In the Old Testament there is another well-known story which sheds light on what happened when Jesus died. God told the prophet Abraham to offer up the son he loved as a sacrifice.[40] God was not planning that Abraham should actually kill his son. Rather he was testing his faith to see how far his obedience would go. So Abraham obeyed God and set out with two of his servants carrying wood to make a burnt offering. At the end of his journey, Abraham left his servants and went on alone with his son. His son was puzzled.

'The fire and wood are here', he said to his father, 'but where is the lamb for the burnt offering?'

Abraham told him that God himself would provide the lamb. Even at that very last moment Abraham did not lose his trust in God. In fact his hand was already raising the knife to sacrifice his son, when the angel of the Lord called out to him from heaven, 'Do not lay a hand on the boy. Now I know that you fear God, because you have not withheld from me your son, your only son.'

Abraham looked up and saw a ram with its horns caught in the nearby bushes. So he sacrificed the ram instead of his son.

In the New Testament we find the same kind of good news that God gave to Abraham on that dramatic day of deliverance. God has provided the final sacrifice for sin in the person of Jesus of

Nazareth! There is no need for any more animal sacrifices, because Jesus gave his life as a full and final sacrifice for all people for all time. This is one of the central messages of the New Testament.

Joseph, the father of Jesus, was told by an angel before Jesus was even born that Jesus would one day 'save his people from their sins'.[41] Another angel appeared to the shepherds near Bethlehem after Jesus was born, saying, 'Today in the town of David a *Saviour* has been born to you; he is Christ (Messiah) the Lord.'[42]

When Simeon, the old man in the temple, held the baby Jesus in his arms he said, 'My eyes have seen your salvation . . .'[43] As Simeon looked at Jesus it was as if he was actually holding God's provision for salvation in his arms.

When John the Baptist looked at Jesus, you will remember he made that extraordinary statement: 'Look, the Lamb of God, who takes away the sin of the world!'[44]

Later on, during the public ministry of Jesus, it is clear that he saw his future death and resurrection as being a sacrifice for sin. Jesus said, 'I am the good shepherd. The good shepherd lays down his life for the sheep . . . no one takes my life from me, but I lay it down of my own accord. I have authority to lay it down and authority to take it up again.'[45]

Here we see that Jesus had complete authority and control over his own destiny. His death was certainly no accident. He knew that he was going to lay his life down for others. This is even clearer in the Passover meal that Jesus had with his disciples just before his death.

But, though Jesus often mentioned *the fact* that his death and resurrection were going to happen, their *meaning* was something he only hinted at. He said, for instance, that his death was to be 'a ransom for many', a means of buying people out of slavery — like the money paid as ransom for a rich man's daughter held by terrorists.

The reason why he did not emphasize the meaning of his coming death and resurrection is simple. There was very little hope of people understanding the death and resurrection of Jesus until after these events had actually happened! Even for Peter it was an immense struggle to accept that Jesus was *both* the

Messiah *and* that he was going to die.[46]

Probably many of those who really believed that Jesus was the Messiah thought that he would be caught up to heaven without dying. They just could not see why he had to die. It was only after the death and resurrection of Jesus that his followers realized the implications of why Jesus really came.

Just a few weeks after these amazing events had taken place, we find Peter preaching to the people that they should repent and believe in Jesus so that their sins might be forgiven.[47] When Peter was arrested and dragged before the Jewish rulers he proclaimed boldly of Jesus that 'Salvation is found in no one else, for there is no other name under heaven given to men by which we must be saved.'[48]

Later on Peter wrote that Jesus had died in perfect fulfilment of the prophecy from Isaiah about the suffering Messiah that we quoted above: 'He committed no sin, and no deceit was found in his mouth', for 'When they hurled their insults at him (Jesus), he did not retaliate; when he suffered, he made no threats . . . he himself bore our sins in his body on the tree, so that we might die to sins and live for righteousness; by his wounds you have been healed.'[49]

'Tree' and 'cross' meant the same thing, because the upright part of the cross was in many cases simply the main trunk of a tree with most of its branches cut off. So, said Peter, the reason that Jesus suffered on the cross was to take away our sins.

But how can a man die to take away the sins of others? Of course that is impossible. One man can never remove the sin of another however noble the method. Only God can take away sin. That is why the claims of Jesus are so crucial. There is no question of Jesus being forsaken by God at the cross, because at the cross God was in Jesus suffering for the sins of mankind. Since man was unable to solve the dilemma of his own sin, God himself took the initiative and came into the world to suffer for us in the person of Jesus.

But why did God do that? Surely as God he could simply forgive anybody who truly repented of their sin? Why was there any need for the cross?

We will never begin to know the answers to these questions unless we understand what God is like. Especially we need to understand the love of God and the justice of God that Jesus taught so clearly.

You will remember that the love of God is *agape* love. It is a quality of love in the person loving. It does not depend on the other person being lovable or attractive in some way, or being able to give something in return. It is a very difficult love for us to understand because it is so foreign to the way that we normally behave. Normally we respond to something about the other person. But God gives to us even when we do not deserve it, when we are not at all lovable and when we can give nothing as a repayment. The New Testament often talks about this aspect of the love of God as the 'grace' of God. The grace of God means God going on giving and giving, more and more.

Jesus on the cross is the supreme expression of God's love for us. When people see war and suffering in the world, they often say 'Why doesn't God *do* something?' The answer is that God *has* done something! At the cross God entered into all the suffering of the world that he had made and himself experienced the agony of death by torture. At the cross God allowed all the sin of the world to roll over Jesus like a mighty wave. Agape love could go no further than that.

But if we are going to understand what happened at the cross, we must also understand the *justice* of God. God is totally just. As he is always loving, so he is always just. The standard for God's justice is his own holiness. His holiness is expressed in the Ten Commandments and in Jesus' Sermon on the Mount (see chapter·three). In fact it is difficult to appreciate God's justice and what he did for us at the cross without reading afresh the Sermon on the Mount. God's plan for the whole human race is that they should follow in the path of true submission to him. But the path of true submission goes right through the Sermon on the Mount. The teachings we find there are what God demands of those who want to be holy. At the end of chapter six we saw this terrible dilemma in which we find ourselves. On one side we see the holiness of God, shining brighter than a thousand suns. On the other side we see mankind completely unable to keep up to the standards of God's holiness. There is nothing that we can *do* ourselves which will change this basic dilemma.

The justice of God is an expression of this holiness. It is not wilful or arbitrary. It is simply that, by definition, nothing dark can live in the light of God's presence, nothing sinful or un-holy can co-exist with his holiness. Sin *must* involve separation — death — a breaking of that fellowship between God and mankind for which mankind was originally designed.

After all, in a court of law we would certainly expect a crime to be punished. We would not expect the judge to deny the whole system of justice by letting a guilty prisoner off completely free. Justice must be done!

Every time we are angry with someone, or lustful, or love money more than God, or practise religious hypocrisy, we fall short of what God demands. We separate ourselves from his holiness. We go our way, not his. There is no way we could pay for all the various ways in which we have fallen short of God's holiness! That kind of punishment would have to go on for ever!

Because God loves us so much, he has opened up a new way for our sins to be forgiven. In the time before Jesus came this was symbolized through animal sacrifice, as we have seen. The pure, innocent animal was taken and its death symbolized the taking away of a person's sin. Of course only God can forgive sin. But when the person sacrificed the animal, they were saying to God that there was no way that they could remove their own sin. They were utterly dependent upon the mercy of God for forgiveness.

When Jesus died, both the love of God and the justice of God were completely demonstrated. God's love was demonstrated because agape love could go no further than the innocent dying for the guilty. God's justice was demonstrated because he accepted in Jesus' death the death of all those who would be bound up with him. God's love and his justice meet at the cross.

There was once a judge who had an elder son whom he loved very much. His elder son had been a responsible member of the family, and his father had looked forward to the day when he would follow in his steps and enter the legal profession. However, his son had rebelled and left home. Imagine the judge's horror when one day his own son was brought before him in court. It appeared that his son had been caught stealing — for which the penalty then was fifty lashes with a whip. Of course the judge could not change the laws so that his son might go free. So he sentenced his son to the just penalty.

After the judge had passed the sentence on his own son, with tears in his eyes he removed his judge's clothes and went down to stand in front of the court. 'Justice must be done!' he cried. 'But also I still love my son, despite all that he has done. So I will take the punishment for him so that he can go free!'

And that is exactly what the judge did. He bared his back and was whipped fifty times before them all. Seeing how much his father loved him, his son repented of all the wrong that he had done and turned away from his life of rebellion. The punishment had been taken. And the son had an inward change of heart. He was brought back into unity with his father.

Our problem is that so many people think they can build their own bridges to God. 'We're not *that* bad,' they say. Or they think they have done their bit to earn their way to heaven. But as we saw in chapter six, our good works and religious observances can never be enough to raise us to the standards of God's holiness. That does not mean that they have no value at all — simply that they are valueless as a bridge to God. It is like a person burning a whole box of matches and then thinking that this will bring them into contact with the sun! For the cancer of sin you need God's much more radical solution, the sacrifice of Jesus on the cross. You may as well give an aspirin for terminal cancer . . .

Much of the teaching of Jesus was centred on the fact that we cannot build our own bridges to God.

Jesus once told a story about a land-owner who hired men early in the morning to work in a vineyard.[50] He agreed on a fixed wage for the day and then sent them out to work. A few hours later he hired a few more workers and told them that he would pay them a just wage as well. All during the day he kept doing this until someone was recruited to work for only the last hour of the day.

At the end of the day the workers all came to receive their wages. The ones who were hired last were paid first. Imagine their surprise when they were given a whole day's pay! Of course the people who had worked longest thought that they would receive much more than this. They were most upset when the land-owner gave them exactly the same pay as the others, in fact just the wage that he had promised them at the beginning of the day. So all the workers received the same pay, even though they had worked for such different lengths of time!

It is not surprising that they grumbled — we would have done the same. But Jesus here is not trying to establish a new wage policy! The real meaning of the story is not about wages at all, but about the priorities of God's kingdom. As Jesus himself concluded at the end of his story, 'The last will be first, and the first will be last.'

Every person in God's kingdom enters on God's terms, not his own. We have no rights that we can demand of God. We have failed miserably to submit even a little to his laws — especially to the law which says that we should love him with all our heart, soul and mind. So God treats everyone the same way. People who think that they most deserve his kingdom find themselves 'last'. The poor, outcast and the rejected — those who have no rights anyway — find to their surprise that they are high on God's list of priorities in his kingdom. God's kingdom turns upside down all our human ideas. All in God's vineyard receive exactly what he has planned for them. The cause for surprise is not that they all receive the same, but that they receive anything at all.

Jesus made a similar point in his famous story about the wedding feast.[51] Jesus said that the kingdom of heaven is like a king who prepared a wedding banquet for his son. He sent out his servants to those who had been invited to the banquet to tell them to come, but they refused. Naturally the man was very upset at this refusal, so he sent more servants to tell the guests that everything was ready. But, shamefully, they still refused to come.

So the king sent out his servants again, this time ordering them to go out in the streets and invite anyone that they found 'both good and bad'. In this way the wedding hall was soon filled with guests. Each guest was given special wedding clothes from the king to wear so that all might be dressed correctly for such a special occasion. But the king noticed that one of the guests was not wearing the wedding clothes that he had provided.

'How did you get in here without wedding clothes?', he asked the man. Then the king told his servants to tie the man up and throw him out into the darkness.

The stories of Jesus are often shocking to us. This one is no exception. It makes us think — always the goal of a good teacher.

Notice first that the people originally invited never came. Jesus is making a special point to the Jewish leaders here. They were so religious that they thought *they* were the chosen ones. But Jesus had made it plain to them that they had completely missed the point of God's kingdom — they had refused the invitation.

In fact God's kingdom was for everyone, for all those who were invited and responded. None were good enough to be in the presence of the king, whether they were 'good or bad'. The only way they could enter the kingdom was by God's grace, by his free gift of a wedding garment. But that was the *only way*. Anyone trying to enter in their own clothes, trusting in what they had in themselves to bring them to the king, would be quickly thrown out.

The cross runs right through the heart of this story of Jesus, because the cross is about people receiving something that they do not deserve. The cross is God's sacrifice for sin for all time, for all people in all places. And the only way we can receive the benefits of that sacrifice is as a gift from God. We cannot earn it.

But you may be saying, 'This is too easy! Is that all we have to do? Just accept what God has done for us with no change in our own lives? Surely this will encourage people to accept the sacrifice of Jesus and then live for themselves?'

To find an answer, we need to look at the resurrection of Jesus and what it means for us today. You will remember that we left the body of Jesus, wrapped in up to 34 kilograms of spices and tightly bound linen in a tomb with a giant stone rolled in front, sealed and guarded by Roman soldiers. What happened next?

How did the resurrection happen?

Jesus died on a Friday. The next day was the Jewish day of rest, the Sabbath. Early the following morning, the third day after Jesus was killed, a group of women went very early in the morning to the tomb of Jesus.[52] Their purpose in going was to anoint the body of Jesus, since there had been no opportunity to do this on the Friday. As they went to the tomb, they wondered how they would be able to move away such a heavy stone.[53] It was clear that they did not believe Jesus was going to rise from the dead — the anointing of the body which they planned to carry out was intended to help preserve it from decay.

When they reached the tomb, they were amazed to find that the heavy stone had been rolled away. There had been a violent earthquake and angels of the Lord had come down from heaven and rolled back the stone.[54]

The women saw one of the angels sitting on the stone. His appearance was like lightning and the Roman guards were scared out of their minds. The angel told the women not to be afraid and informed them that Jesus had risen from the dead. As they could see for themselves, he was no longer in the tomb! The women must go quickly and tell his disciples of what had happened. The angels had not rolled the stone to let Jesus out, but so that the women could look in and see that the tomb really was empty!

As they were returning to the city, Jesus himself suddenly appeared to them. They fell to the ground and worshipped him.[55] Jesus also made a special appearance to Mary Magdala.[56] She was a woman from whom Jesus had once driven seven demons. So Jesus appeared first to the least valued people in society — a group of women — and picked especially one who had been totally without hope before he had released her from satanic powers.

Probably the women had come to the tomb first because they also felt more free to move in and out of the city. Jesus had just been tortured to death. No doubt his close disciples thought that they would be the next on the list. But for the women it was different. It was men who were seen as political agitators — generally women would be left alone during such times of tension and trouble.

In fact the men were so frightened that only two of the disciples dared go to the tomb to check on the extraordinary news that the women had told them. The disciples did not believe the women anyway and thought they were talking nonsense! So it was just Peter and John who set out for the tomb.[57] Just as the women had said, the tomb was clearly empty. They went right inside and saw the burial linen, flattened by the weight of the spices and lying in two sections. The main section had surrounded the body of Jesus. A separate part had been wrapped around his head. Now just the wrappings were left, lying like the chrysalis of a moth after it has turned into a butterfly. There was no body inside. As

Jesus had risen, his resurrection body had passed right through the linen, leaving it undisturbed.

That same Sunday, two other disciples of Jesus were walking to a village outside Jerusalem called Emmaus.[58] They were probably returning home following their attendance at the Passover feast. As they walked, Jesus came up and started walking with them. But at first they did not recognize him! In fact they were not from the inner circle of the twelve disciples of Jesus.

As Jesus walked with them, they began to tell him of how Jesus of Nazareth, 'a prophet in word and deed' had been crucified that very week. The two disciples had already heard how the women had reported that the tomb was empty, and how this had been verified by Peter and John. But they seemed to be puzzled as to what this meant.

'We had hoped', they said, 'that Jesus was the one who was going to redeem Israel.'

So they were still thinking that Jesus was some kind of political saviour, sent to rescue the nation of Israel from her political enemies. People always have a problem seeing that true religion goes beyond the boundaries of their own nation or community.

The living, resurrected Jesus who walked beside these two disciples was very blunt about their limited view of who he really was.

'How foolish you are', he said to them, 'and how slow of heart to believe all that the prophets have spoken!'

Then Jesus went on to explain to them that he was really the Messiah, and his whole purpose in coming into the world had not been to save one nation, but to suffer for everybody.

As they finally entered the village of Emmaus together, the two disciples invited Jesus in for a meal, still not recognizing who he was. It was only when they were sitting at the table together and Jesus was giving thanks for the food, that they suddenly recognized him!

Perhaps carrying out the familiar act of giving thanks for food helped the disciples to recognize Jesus. If you have ever met someone that you do not know well in a totally unexpected setting, then you will understand how easy it is not to recognize them. These two disciples were certainly not hallucinating. The conditions were exactly the opposite from what you would expect for a hallucination. It was not that they were expecting to see Jesus — this might have generated an actual vision by wish fulfilment. Instead they were *not* expecting to see him, and that critical non-expectancy clouded their recognition until Jesus was actually sitting with them in their home.

As soon as Jesus had disappeared from their sight, the two disciples went hurrying back to Jerusalem to tell the eleven main disciples (there were now only eleven because Judas had committed suicide). But they found the disciples already largely convinced that Jesus had risen because by that time Jesus had already appeared to Simon Peter.[59] So the disciples had not listened to the women seriously, but they did respect Peter!

While they were still talking together, Jesus himself stood among them and said, 'Peace be with you.'[60]

The disciples were startled and frightened, thinking that they were seeing a ghost. But Jesus told them to look at his hands and his feet, which still bore the scars of his crucifixion. He told his disciples to touch him and prove it for themselves: 'A ghost does not have flesh and bones, as you see I have!' To underline this, he took a piece of broiled fish and ate it in their presence.

The resurrection body of Jesus was a very real body. He was no phantom. At the same time it is clear that his body had different properties from an ordinary body. For example, he could pass right through doors and walls, appearing and disappearing as he wished.

There was one disciple who was not present when Jesus appeared to the other disciples at this time. His name was Thomas. You may remember that he was the one with the rather sceptical temperament. When the other disciples told Thomas that they had seen the risen Jesus, he simply would not believe it.[61]

'Unless I see the nail marks in his hands', said Thomas, 'and put my finger where the nails were, and put my hand into his side, I will not believe it.'

A week later Thomas was with the other disciples and the doors were locked, because they were still very scared of what the Jewish authorities would do next. Suddenly Jesus came again and stood among them. Then he said to Thomas, 'Put your finger here; see my hands. Reach out your hand and put it into my side. Stop doubting and believe.'

Thomas answered, 'My Lord and my God!'

Then Jesus told him, 'Because you have seen me, you have believed; blessed are those who have not seen and yet have believed.'

Like Thomas, we might naturally feel sceptical about claims that Jesus died and rose from the dead. Yet if *we* were able to watch Jesus die, running our finger down the cross so that we had splinters in it, and then meet and touch the resurrected Jesus a few days later — we would believe too! But Jesus said that we are more blessed if we have *not* seen the historical event itself. Instead we have to look at the evidence. We have to read what the eyewitnesses wrote. We have to consider what other possibilities there might be to explain what had happened. Then we have to decide for ourselves.

It was the Jewish leaders who made up the first alternative story to explain away the resurrection of Jesus. Just after Jesus had risen, the guards who had been posted at his tomb went and told the chief priests what had happened.[62] They were probably Roman soliders, but they went to the Jewish authorities rather than to the Roman governor Pilate for the simple reason that the punishment for negligence in the Roman army was instant death. It is interesting that the Jewish authorities made no attempt to deny the soldiers' story. Instead they bribed them with a large sum of money and instructed them to say, 'His disciples came during the night and stole him away while we were asleep.'

This was the story that began to circulate among the Jews. But as an explanation it has no historical foundation. In the first place the disciples had been so frightened when Jesus had been arrested that they had all run off and left him. It is hardly likely that, unarmed, they would have been able to overpower the heavily armed Roman soldiers and steal the body. In fact they were staying in their locked houses and hardly dared go out!

And if they had stolen the body, where did they put it? The Roman authorities had very firm control on the area. If the body of Jesus was placed in another tomb, why is it that this never became a place of pilgrimage for his followers, as has happened with the tombs of other great religious leaders of the world?

Moreover, if the disciples stole the body, why did they soon begin to preach so strongly in the streets that Jesus was risen? Later on many of the followers of Jesus were tortured to death for their faith because they refused to deny him. Psychologically, how could they be willing to die for something that they knew deep inside them was a lie?

The greatest evidence for the resurrection is that Jesus appeared to so many people at different times. A few people with a certain kind of personality might be deceived once, but many varied people over a period of a few weeks saw the risen Jesus. Not many believed in him when they saw the empty tomb, because not many understood what it meant. But they certainly believed when they saw the risen Messiah.

For example, Jesus later appeared to seven of his disciples by the Sea of Galilee. During this time he ate breakfast with them and spent some special time in challenging and building up the faith of Peter.[63] On another occasion he appeared to more than 500 people at the same time. One other time Jesus appeared personally to James.[64]

The resurrection of Jesus is not just a nice story, a legend that grew up to express people's admiration for Jesus, some kind of wish-fulfilment. It is not the claim that Jesus somehow 'lives on' in his teachings which are still widely taught and accepted by many. Neither is it the claim that the spirit of Jesus is alive while his bones lie rotting in a cave just outside Jerusalem. Rather it is the declaration that Jesus himself has risen from the dead with a new resurrection body. Jesus lives, and death can never again have any power over him.

Why did Jesus rise from the dead?

In fact, Jesus had to rise from the dead! How could death hold him?

Death could certainly not hold Jesus if his claims are true. If Jesus is the Messiah, the Son of Man, spiritually continuous with God himself, then clearly there was no way he could stay in that tomb longer than was necessary to fulfil God's plan of salvation. God is the source of life. Death has no more ultimate claim on

God than the moon has during its temporary eclipse of the sun. Eclipse may last for a short while, but you can be very sure that the light will soon return.

Jesus experienced real death because that was the only way that there could be a full and final sacrifice for human sin. But because he was sinless, death had no power over him. Death has power only where there is sin. Jesus did not die for his own sin but for the sin of others. So death had no ultimate grip upon him.

Imagine that there is a race of beings on another planet. They live under the constant control of deadly rays which come from a giant beam set in the heart of their planet. The beam was put there by an evil power soon after their race first began. The rays were tuned by this evil power to penetrate into certain sensitive areas of their brains. So everything that they think, say and do is affected by the rays. No one can turn the dreadful beam off, because the closer they come to the source of the beam, the more they are repelled by it. The situation seems hopeless.

Then one day someone comes from another planet whose brain is not affected by the rays. The people are all amazed. How can someone live among them in the presence of the terrible rays and yet be so joyful, fulfilled and full of power? The simple fact is that the rays have no hold on him — his brain has never experienced them before, and he is able to resist the rays.

The Man from outside proclaims to the people that they can be free from the dreaded rays. He even demonstrates that freedom by his own life and works. The people are impressed, but do not themselves have the power to change.

Finally the Man goes right to the source of the beam. The beam does not repel him as it does the others, but the closer he gets to the source, the more excruciating is the pain because of the intensity of the rays. But because of his love for the others, he does not give up. At last the Man reaches the source of the beam and destroys it by throwing himself upon it, dying in agony in the process.

Once the source of the rays has been destroyed, they no longer have power over the Man, and he rises from the dead. But there is one last problem. The rays will continue to reflect around the planet for a long time. Because their source is destroyed they have nothing like the power they had before. But they are still a problem. Only those who come to the Man and allow him to change that sensitive area in their brains so that they are no longer under the grip of those reflected rays can be free. One day even the reflected rays will disappear, but that day is not yet.

This is just a story. It is not intended to illustrate all that happened through the death and resurrection of Jesus! But I hope that it will help clarify a few points.

Through the death and resurrection of Jesus, not only the penalty but also the power of sin was broken. Sin is everything that drags us down, all that pulls us away from God. Jesus has destroyed the source of the cancer of sin once and for all. At the cross he took the penalty of our sin as a sacrifice. As he rose from the dead he demonstrated that Satan is a defeated enemy. The source of evil itself was crushed. Satan still has some power remaining while we live in the present world of time. But his days are numbered. One day the last remnants of his power will be destroyed.

So the death and resurrection of Jesus are God's radical remedy for the terrible 'disease' of sin that we looked at in chapter six. As we look at the empty tomb, we see that God has done the impossible, powerfully overcoming the results of sin and at the same time crushing Satan's grip on the world.

We can now see why Jesus is always the focal point of the kingdom of God in the New Testament. As Jesus rose victoriously from the dead, he rose as a conquering king. He was not a political king who had defeated the power of Rome, but he was a Messianic king who had destroyed the very roots of men and women's alienation from God, from each other, and from themselves.

From that moment on there was nothing that could hold back God's reign — his kingdom. It is therefore no surprise that Jesus told his disciples very soon after his resurrection that their task was now to proclaim the message of the kingdom all over the world:

> All authority in heaven and on earth has been given to me. Therefore go and make disciples of all nations, baptising them in the name of the Father and of the Son and of the Holy Spirit, and teaching them to obey everything I have

commanded you. And surely I will be with you always, to the very end of the age.[65]

Notice that the command Jesus gave to his disciples was not to go and try to change people's religion. That would be futile! When someone enters the kingdom of God they are not 'changing their religion'. In fact Jesus taught very clearly that following certain religious observances was *never* enough for someone to go to heaven. There was no point in people substituting one set of religious rules for another — in that case they would be in just the same position as before.

No, what the disciples were to do was to proclaim the true path of submission to God through Jesus. The word 'baptism' literally means 'dipping', 'submersing' or 'burying'. When a ship sank in the sea it was said to be 'baptized' in the sea. So for a person coming to believe in Jesus is like being immersed, drowned — and then reborn. They share in the death of Jesus — *and* in his new life. It means accepting Jesus as king, as the one who from then on is going to lead and control that person's life. It involves allowing the resurrection power of Jesus to flood in, destroying the old and building up the new.

This is why accepting the salvation which God is offering to us through the death and resurrection of Jesus is never easy. First, it is not easy because it means admitting that we need God's help — there is nothing we can do to change ourselves. If we try to come to God depending on our own efforts, then we are sure to fail. Accepting the free gift of salvation which God is offering to us hurts our pride. We would much prefer to earn our own salvation and be rewarded for our labour. It is much harder for our pride to receive something as a gift than to work for it.

Second, accepting the results of the death and resurrection of Jesus into our own life is not easy because it involves accepting the full power of God himself in our life. That is a dangerous step to take! It means that we are willing for God to change us and mould us according to the ethics of the kingdom of God which Jesus taught. It means that we are willing for God to start cleaning out those dark areas of our lives which we would prefer no one else knew about. It means a total reordering of our priorities so that 'King-Self' is no longer in the centre of our lives, but rather 'King-Jesus' has the central place.

Imagine hundreds of fish swimming down river, carried comfortably along by the strong current. Suddenly a single fish turns around and starts swimming up stream, trying to return to the source of the river itself. That is not an easy step to take! Both the strong current and the other fish are against him. So it is for anybody who turns to swim against the stream by believing in Jesus.

The third reason why such a crucial step is a hard one is because it involves waging war on Satan himself. Satan's power and authority have been broken through the sacrifice of Jesus on the cross. But he is still very active in the world, and when we accept God's kingdom of light, it is like declaring war on Satan. Once we accept the resurrected Jesus as king, then a battle begins to take place in our lives. It is the battle between light and darkness.

Just as Jesus himself clashed with demonic powers when he was here on earth, so that clash continues as his resurrection power enters our lives and confronts all that is evil in us. Anyone trusting in charms, amulets, spells or the power of the evil eye to protect them will have to throw them away. Those playing with ouija boards and other occult practices will have to stop them. People going to mediums for advice or taking part in seances will have to give up these practices. You cannot have light and darkness existing in the same place simultaneously.

Flying the new flag of the kingdom is not going to be easy. Living out the values of the kingdom — that is tough. Yet God demands no less for those who wish to share in the death and resurrection of Jesus of Nazareth.

But praise God, he has also given us a new power to live out his kingdom. He has given us his Holy Spirit in order to make this way possible for people in their daily lives. Just how the Holy Spirit makes a dramatic difference when he enters someone's life, we must now go on to consider.

1 Luke 9:21–22
2 Matthew 16:23
3 Luke 9:51
4 Luke 13:31

5   Luke 13:33
6   Matthew 21:9
7   Matthew 24 – 25; John 14 – 16
8   Exodus 12:12–13
9   John 1:29
10 Matthew 26:28
11 Matthew 27:3–4
12 Matthew 26:63
13 Luke 22:70–71
14 Matthew 26:61
15 Luke 23:1–6
16 Luke 23:8–12
17 Matthew 27:17
18 Matthew 27:24–26
19 Matthew 27:27–31
20 Matthew 27:32
21 Matthew 27:34
22 Luke 23:35
23 Matthew 27:42–43
24 John 19:25
25 John 19:26
26 Luke 23:39–43
27 John 19:30
28 Matthew 27:51
29 John 19:31
30 John 19:33–35
31 Luke 23:50–54
32 John 3:1, 19:39–40
33 Matthew 27:59–60; John 19:41
34 Matthew 27:62–66
35 Mark 14:63–64
36 John 19:7
37 Mark 14:66–72
38 1 Peter 2:21
39 Isaiah 53:3, 5–7, 9, 12
40 Genesis 22:1–14
41 Matthew 1:21
42 Luke 2:11
43 Luke 2:30

44 John 1:29
45 John 10:11, 18
46 Matthew 20:28; Mark 10:45
47 Acts 2:38
48 Acts 4:12
49 1 Peter 2:22–24
50 Matthew 20:1–16
51 Matthew 22:1–14
52 Matthew 28:1; Mark 16:1–3; Luke 24:1–3; John 20:1–2
53 Mark 16:3
54 Matthew 28:2–4
55 Matthew 28:8–9
56 Mark 16:9; John 20:10–18
57 Luke 24:11–12; John 20:3–9
58 Luke 24:13–35
59 Luke 24:33–34
60 Luke 24:36–44
61 John 20:24–29
62 Matthew 28:11–15
63 John 21:1–24
64 1 Corinthians 15:3–8
65 Matthew 28:18–20

The Ascension and Coming Again of Jesus

Forty days after rising from the dead, Jesus ascended to heaven.[1] During those few weeks he appeared on many occasions to his disciples and taught them much. His teaching focused especially on the meaning of God's kingdom. It was far easier for his followers to understand the reign of God now that Jesus had conquered the great enemies of sin and death.

Jesus also helped his disciples to see how his life and death had been in fulfilment of the Old Testament writings. He explained to them that the reason for his sufferings was for 'repentance and forgiveness of sins' which now would be 'preached in his name to all nations.'[2]

That in itself must have been a shocking revelation to Jesus' disciples. They had only slowly begun to realize while living with Jesus that he had certainly not come to liberate one small community. Now they were faced with the challenge of taking the message of God's kingdom to the whole world. To a small group of uncultured Galilean fishermen, that command of Jesus was quite a challenge!

Just before he ascended to heaven, Jesus gave strict instructions to his disciples that they were to wait in Jerusalem until they were 'clothed with power from on high' and 'baptized with the Holy Spirit'.[3] The disciples must have been very curious to know what this might involve, because several times before his death Jesus had told them that he was going to send the Holy Spirit.

Who or what was this Holy Spirit?

Jesus had explained to his disciples that the Holy Spirit was the power of God himself released into people's lives to perform the works of God. So Jesus had even said that it was for 'their good' that he was leaving them.[4] It was only after he had conquered sin and death through his death and resurrection that the Holy Spirit would come. The Holy Spirit would be like having Jesus himself living inside them.[5]

Jesus had told them, 'I will not leave you as orphans; I will come to you. Before long, the world will not see me any more, but you will see me. Because I live, you also will live.'[6]

Jesus had no intention of leaving his followers trying to live out the life of God's kingdom in their own strength. He knew that was only possible with God's power. So he had told his disciples that his Holy Spirit would teach them all they needed to know.[7] The Holy Spirit would make their words powerful as they told others about Jesus.[8] The Holy Spirit would show people how deep was their sin as their lives were compared to the standards of God's holiness.[9] The Holy Spirit would bring the very will and power of God into the centre of the lives of those who chose the way of true submission.

Exactly forty days after his resurrection, Jesus led his disciples to the area of Bethany, about 3 kilometres from Jerusalem. Bethany was the village where Jesus had stayed with Simon the leper just before his death. It was also the place where he had raised Lazarus from the dead and where Mary the sister of Lazarus had anointed the feet of Jesus. It was an area which had so many vivid associations for the disciples. The village represented a cross-section of needy people who had been made whole through God's kingdom.

So it was surely no accident that Jesus chose the area of Bethany from which to ascend to heaven. As he arrived with his disciples, Jesus lifted up his hands and blessed them. Then he was taken up directly into heaven and a cloud hid him from their sight. This does not imply that heaven is 'up', somewhere 'beyond the sky'. It was an obvious picture of Jesus leaving earth and going to heaven, a different order of existence, the presence of God. So in our scientific age there is no need to feel superior about this vivid story. No doubt we still talk about the sun 'rising' like anyone else!

The disciples were still staring into heaven when two men dressed in white appeared to them.

'Men of Galilee', they said, 'why do you stand here looking

into the sky? This same Jesus, who has been taken from you into heaven, will come back in the same way you have seen him go into heaven.'[10]

There are many people today who believe that Jesus is indeed in heaven, but that God could not have forsaken Jesus on the cross, and so God took Jesus to heaven before he died. But, as we have seen, Jesus *did* die — and rose triumphantly from the grave before returning in glory to heaven. It was the *task* of the Messiah to die as a sacrifice for sin. What God wills to do, he always accomplishes. There is nothing incomplete in the works of the all-powerful God. Would Jesus return to heaven before finishing all that God had planned?

After the ascension the disciples returned to Jerusalem. Considering the final command that Jesus had given them, we might have expected them to go immediately out into the streets and preach the message of God's kingdom to the people. But they did not. Instead they spent much time together worshipping God in the temple.[11] They also appointed a man to replace Judas, who was to be a man, like them, who had personally witnessed the resurrection of Jesus.[12]

By this time the disciples knew why Jesus had come. They knew why he had died and risen from the dead. They had listened to his command to tell others about God's kingdom. But at first they did nothing about it! They had all the right beliefs, but not the *power* to put those beliefs into action.

The gift of the Holy Spirit

Ten days after Jesus had ascended into heaven, the disciples were gathered together in Jerusalem. It was the time of the Jewish festival called the Feast of Weeks, or Pentecost. Suddenly a sound like a violent wind came from heaven and filled the whole house where they were sitting, and tongues of fire came to rest over each one of the disciples.[13] All of them were filled with the Holy Spirit and began to speak in other tongues.

You may remember from chapter two that as John the Baptist had prepared the way for Jesus, he had told people that Jesus was the one who was going to 'baptize them with the Holy Spirit and with fire'.[14] As we have seen, 'baptize' means 'bury' or 'immerse'. So being 'baptized with the Holy Spirit' meant being 'immersed' in the very power of God himself. For the disciples it was the moment in time when theory became practice. Before that they knew what they should do. Now they had the power to do it.

Fire represented the cleansing, purifying aspect of God's holiness. As the Holy Spirit came on the disciples, it was as if God was clearing out all the impurities of their old lives and was filling them with his new life of holiness. They were filled with the *Holy* Spirit of God. Wherever God is really at work, there you find holiness.

There were thousands of visitors from many Middle Eastern nations crowded into Jerusalem at that time for the feast. As they heard the roar of the wind rushing through the house, they quickly gathered in the area. All were bewildered to hear the disciples speaking to them in their own language. There were people there from Turkey, Egypt, various parts of North Africa, Rome, and many other places. They knew that people from Galilee were the most uneducated men in Palestine, yet they were amazed to hear them speaking all their different languages! So God gave a clear sign to everybody that the work of his Spirit was intended for all people from all nations.

As the crowd grew, the people became even more curious. Then the disciples began to do something that they had never dared to do before. They began to preach openly to the crowds about the risen Jesus. It was Peter who first stood up boldly to address the crowd — the very same Peter who had completely denied Jesus just a few weeks earlier!

Peter told the people that the giving of the Holy Spirit had been prophesied long before in the Old Testament.[15] The prophet Joel had foretold hundreds of years before that one day God would pour out his Spirit on *all* those who really believed in him. That day, said Peter, had now arrived, 'and *everyone* who calls on the name of the Lord will be saved.'

Peter went on to explain to the crowds that the giving of the Holy Spirit had been made possible through the death and resurrection of Jesus.[16] Jesus had smashed down the wall of sin separating God and man. Now it was possible for anyone to know God and for the life-giving power of God himself — his Spirit — to come into their lives and turn them upside down.

The people were deeply moved as they heard Peter preaching and asked what they should do.

'Repent and be baptised, every one of you', said Peter, 'in the name of Jesus Christ so that your sins may be forgiven. And you will receive the gift of the Holy Spirit. The promise is for you and your children and for all who are far off — for all whom the Lord our God will call.'[17]

Repentance meant that the people had to turn away from their old life of sin and turn to Jesus, to the light and power of God's kingdom. It meant that they had to be genuinely sorry for the many ways in which they had broken God's commandments. They had to be willing for a complete change of direction in their lives.

Being 'baptized' meant being immersed in water as a vivid symbol of the inner change that God was bringing about in the life by his Holy Spirit. As those who really repented and turned from their sin were 'baptized' or 'immersed' in God's Spirit, so being 'baptized' in water was an outward sign of this inward revolution. Water was a symbol of cleansing then as it is today. The Holy Spirit cleansed and washed away the sin of those who repented. As they went down into a river, pool or bath to be baptized, it was as if their old life was being buried. As they came out from the water, it was a vivid picture of rising again with Jesus to a new life of power in which sin and Satan would no longer have control over their lives.

It was not the act of baptism itself that saved the people who repented. There was nothing magic about going under the water. Rather the baptism was like the ring on the finger of someone who had just been married. It is by the marriage promises that a person is actually married to someone else. But it would be strange to have no ring placed on the finger as a result of those promises. The ring is a vivid symbol to the watching world of a new step which has been taken, a new relationship which has begun. So it is with baptism.

Notice that Peter talked about receiving the *gift* of the Holy Spirit. As we have noticed before, there is nothing that we can do to earn God's salvation. Salvation is a gift. If I take some money out of my pocket and give it to you, that is a gift. If you work for it, then it can no longer be a gift — instead it becomes a reward or a wage.

Because he loves *all* people from *all* nations so much, God is offering all those who really repent of their sin free forgiveness and the free gift of his Holy Spirit to change their lives and make them holy.

Let us never think that this is an easy step to take. Imagine inviting a king to come and stay with you. It is easy to ask him into your home. But once the king has entered, the cost of giving hospitality to your guest is enormous! Everything in your home must be at his disposal. All your wealth, food and time must be given up to honouring your royal visitor.

So it is when someone asks King Jesus into their lives. He comes in by his Spirit quite freely. But his presence costs everything that person is and has. That is what God's kingdom is all about.

Those who repented and received the gift of the Holy Spirit as Peter was preaching soon found this out for themselves. There were about 3,000 of them who became followers of Jesus on that first day.[18] Many would have been people who had seen Jesus before his death and were already familiar with his teachings.

Those who received the Holy Spirit soon found that it was just as Jesus had foretold — what Jesus had done on earth himself was now being reproduced inside them by his Spirit. They were no longer living according to their own strength, but by God's power.

So they began to be able to do miracles of healing. Soon after receiving the Holy Spirit, Peter healed a man who had been a cripple from birth 'in the name of Jesus the Messiah of Nazareth'.[19] Just as when Jesus had healed people, the immediate result of the miracle was that both the man and the people around gave praise to God. In fact the man went with Peter and John into the temple 'walking and jumping, and praising God!' He was so happy to be healed! You can always know if a miracle really is from God because if it is, then it will result in God himself being praised and honoured, not the man who did it.

Just as Jesus had great courage and boldness during his public ministry, so now the Holy Spirit gave to the disciples a boldness which they had never experienced before. Repeatedly they were arrested, imprisoned and beaten by the Jewish authorities.[20] Yet nothing could stop them telling everyone about the true meaning of the death and resurrection of Jesus. Soon some began to be executed for their faith, but still they kept on.

Those who received the Holy Spirit also began to experience the 'fruits' of God's Spirit. You can know a tree by the fruit it bears. A tree does not struggle to produce its fruit. Rather the fruit appears naturally as the tree puts its roots deep in the soil and draws up the right nourishment. So the fruits of God's Spirit are those qualities which reflect God's holiness and are produced by the power of God himself in someone's life. The apostle Paul later listed them: 'The fruit of the Spirit is love, joy, peace, patience, kindness, goodness, faithfulness, gentleness and self-control.'[21]

This is exactly the fruit which began to appear in the lives of those who had received God's Spirit. Before they had been a quarrelsome bunch of people, often fighting about who would be the greatest. Now they really began to show real *agape love*. At the beginning, while the new community was relatively small, all the believers had everything in common.[22] They sold their possessions and gave to the poor.

At the same time they began to experience a supernatural joy which was not just present when things were going well. After the disciples had been beaten by the authorities, we read that 'they rejoiced because they had been counted worthy of suffering disgrace for the name (of Jesus).'[23]

Even in prison they experienced a deep peace, so much so that they could sing hymns of praise to God even while they sat in the darkness of a filthy cell, with their feet fixed firmly so that they could not move.[24] Stephen, the first to be killed for his faith, prayed for his executors as they stoned him to death, just as Jesus had prayed for those responsible for his death.[25]

So it really was like having Jesus living right inside them. It was as if he was continuing his own kingdom work on earth by being the new, powerful king of their lives.

At the same time the *gifts* of the Holy Spirit were given so that people would be more effective in their service of others. Some of these gifts were quite dramatic, like the gift of healing, and the

gift of tongues which had been given as the Holy Spirit first came
with the wind and fire. Other gifts were much less spectacular but
no less important, such as gifts of teaching, hospitality and
administration.

The fruits, the gifts and the power of the Spirit were all results
of God's kingdom power. Just as Jesus had broken into the
world by preaching and demonstrating the power of God's reign
as he cast out demons and healed the sick, so now his kingdom
power spread out from Jerusalem like ripples in a lake after a
stone has been dropped. As more and more people experienced
forgiveness from sin through the death and resurrection of Jesus,
so they too entered God's kingdom and began to experience his
kingly power in their lives.

At first the preaching of the disciples was mainly among the
Jews. But then it spread to the Samaritans,[26] and very soon the
message of God's kingdom was moving out among the non-
Jewish nations around.[27] The message was called the 'Gospel',
'Injil' or 'Good News' — the fact that God had come into the
world in Jesus to deliver anyone who really repented from their
slavery to sin and death, and to give them a new life full of God's
kingdom power which will be brought about by his Spirit.

The Trinity

I have not used the term 'the Trinity' so far in this book for the
simple reason that it is not a word found in the New Testament.
Indeed it is quite possible to be a follower of Jesus and not use the
word at all.

One aspect of the word 'Trinity' which many find offensive or
shocking is that it comes from a Latin word meaning 'three'.
When the word is used about God, it therefore sometimes gives
the idea that followers of Jesus believe in three gods. I hope you
have seen by now that this idea is totally wrong. Jesus himself and
all his true followers in the 2,000 years since he lived on earth
have always believed in one God. So how did the idea arise that
there is diversity within the oneness of God?

As we have seen, a group of monotheistic Jews began to live
with Jesus for a few years, and were so overwhelmed by his

power, character and miracles, that they came to believe he was spiritually continuous in some sense with God himself. This belief was confirmed when Jesus died, rose from the dead and ascended into heaven right before their eyes. The belief was expressed through many terms that Jesus used about himself, such as Messiah, Son of Man and Son of God. None of these terms in themselves gives us the complete picture about Jesus, but when we take them all together, we can begin to build up an accurate idea of who Jesus claimed to be. That picture certainly includes the concept that Jesus was continuous with God the Father in heaven while he was here on earth.

I tried to suggest in chapter seven, through the illustration of Flat-land and the three red rings, that it is useless for us to try to understand God himself completely. A fly may as well try to understand a computer! The important point is to understand why we cannot understand, to realize there are limits to our knowledge of God, and to remember that we have finite brains in time and space struggling to comprehend the eternal.

When doubting Thomas fell at the feet of the risen Jesus and cried 'My Lord and my God' he was not making a philosophical statement. Rather, it was an act of worship as he experienced his risen Saviour for himself.

To the astonishment of the disciples, that personal experience of the risen Messiah continued even after Jesus had ascended into heaven. When the Holy Spirit was given, it was as if Jesus had come to live right inside them. The Holy Spirit produced in action on earth the works of Jesus in heaven, and so the will of the Father in heaven.

Therefore the 'threeness' in the oneness of God's being began not as some philosophical speculation, but as a direct result of the experience in history of the disciples as they knew the reality of both Jesus and, later on, the Holy Spirit. As God the Father, God the Son and God the Holy Spirit were equally doing the works of God, so all were expressing the unity of God, not his disunity.

The distinctiveness of the three is not that their status or 'level' is any different, rather that their roles in the salvation of man are distinctive. The 'model' of God the Father expresses that great love of God for the whole of suffering mankind. This involved God the Son being born into the world as the Messiah in order to die and rise again for the sin of mankind. This in turn involved God the Spirit reproducing the new life of God's kingdom in the communities of those who put their faith in him.

That is why you will find true followers of Jesus today who are continuing the historical experience which the early disciples had. As doubting Thomas shouted 'My Lord and my God', so believers today do not hesitate to pray to Jesus in heaven as God. They experience the power, fruit and gifts of the Holy Spirit in their daily lives in the same way that the first disciples did.

As far as the word 'Trinity' is concerned, the problem came when the message of the kingdom spread out to many Greek-speaking areas of the Roman Empire. Although Greece itself had been conquered by the Roman Empire, Greek culture still had an enormous influence throughout the Near East.

During the centuries after the life of Jesus, there was increasing pressure in the Greek-speaking world to give precise philo-sophical definitions to the nature of God. This led to competing schools of thought, which often differed over tiny unimportant points of definition. As the rival statements about God became more and more detailed and controversial, more attuned to Greek thought than the Hebrew roots of Christianity, so the people themselves moved away from the dynamic love and power of God's kingdom. They no longer experienced that fulness of the Holy Spirit which had enabled the early disciples to live out on earth the life of the heavenly Jesus. Instead their beliefs became more and more abstract and philosophical. In the place of a living relationship with God they substituted religious rules and regulations, so making Christianity into just another religion.

We have already seen that it is quite impossible to make precise definitions about the being of God. So we are on much safer ground if we concentrate instead on looking at his great saving acts in history.

Even with a human being on earth you can only really under-stand what that person is like inside by watching what they *do*. This gives us a clue about how to increase our understanding of the one true God. We have to look at what God has *done* in history and what he is longing to do now in our own lives, if only we will let him.

The reality which the word 'Trinity' is supposed to summarize can only be experienced by the person who follows in the footsteps of the first disciples of Jesus. The disciples responded to the amazing love of God the Father as God the Son came into the world to die for the sin of mankind, so opening the way for God the Spirit to make God's kingdom real in the hearts of those who repented. The way to know God is to follow in the same path.

Sadly today there are millions of people calling themselves Christians who know nothing of God's power in their lives. They are not real followers of Jesus. You can easily tell who *is* a true follower because, over a period of time, the fruit of the Holy Spirit will be evident in the person's life. Of course he or she will not be perfect, but that fruit is always a reliable sign of the presence of God's kingdom.

In every generation there are those who leave the dead formality of religious rules and return to the New Testament itself to learn about the dynamic, revolutionary way which Jesus taught. It is that revolution of love which is sweeping the world as the coming again of Jesus draws closer.

The second coming of Jesus

Jesus promised many times that he was going to come again. But he said that his second coming would be quite different from his first. The first time he came, it was as a baby in Bethlehem in his role as the suffering Messiah. But the second would be in the clouds of heaven as a conquering King.

We have already seen that just after the ascension of Jesus, two angels told the disciples that Jesus would come back from heaven in the same way as they had seen him go into heaven. It was going to be a public event.

Jesus himself made this quite clear in his teaching. He once said that 'as lightning comes from the east and flashes to the west, so will be the coming of the Son of Man'.[28]

There is nothing secret about lightning! Jesus foretold that false prophets would come claiming to be the Messiah, but it would be easy to know they were false because they would not come like lightning, visible to everyone.[29]

So there is no idea in the teaching of Jesus that he will some-how return secretly and then proclaim himself as the returned Messiah. Instead his second coming will be so dramatic that no one will have any doubts about what is happening: 'The sign of the Son of Man will appear in the sky, and all the nations of the earth will mourn. They will see the Son of Man coming on the clouds of the sky, with power and great glory.'[30]

What will Jesus do when he comes again? As he comes, he will send his angels to gather all those who believe in him and take them to heaven.[31] At the same time there will be a general resur-rection of all those who have died, 'For a time is coming', said Jesus, 'when all who are in the graves will hear his voice and come out — those who have done good will rise to live and those who have done evil will rise to be condemned.'[32]

Then Jesus the King will bring all the nations before him, 'sitting on his throne in heavenly glory', and the great judgment will begin. As people have judged and criticized others, so they will be judged.[33] Not a word of anger, not a lustful look, not a taste of revenge nor a heart full of pride will escape the blinding light of God's holiness on that day.[34] Religious hypocrites will have their evil exposed as if they had suddenly become trans-parent. Every giving of false change, every cheating in exams, every lie, every moment of jealousy, every false boast will be brought to the bar of God's justice. Murderers will tremble. Those who shed innocent blood to achieve political goals will have to give account for every drop spilt.

If God holds a balance on that great day, then we will all stand condemned. We have already seen that no amount of good works can ever be sufficient to bridge the gap which separates us from a holy God.

But all those who have already been freed in this life from the guilt of their sin through the death and resurrection of Jesus will be saved from condemnation on that judgment day. As the great list of accusations is read out, those people will cry, 'Yes, it is all true! We know that we have fallen far short of God's holiness. We deserve nothing but hell! But we are trusting in that great sacrifice of Jesus on the cross by which we have already received forgiveness. Praise God for that great gift of salvation!' And the great judge will save them from eternal condemnation as they go to be with their Lord for ever.

For those who never entered God's kingdom on this earth there will be eternal punishment in hell. Jesus made quite clear that hell was not preparation for heaven. Rather it meant eternal separation from God. Those who did not show the evidence of the kingdom in their lives 'will go away to eternal punishment, but the righteous to eternal life'.[35]

The decisions we make in this life are eternal in their results. Once we have made our final decision to live apart from the new kingdom life that God is offering to us, then God respects our decision and allows us to keep going on our own way apart from him for all eternity. He never forces himself into our lives. Love never forces.

Jesus did not tell us in detail what heaven or hell would be like. But he made it clear that the focal point of heaven would be the presence of God himself. Jesus taught that he had come from heaven and was returning to heaven. He said that eternal life begins immediately for the person who truly knows God.[36] Heaven is a fulfilment of that eternal life.

In other parts of the New Testament we are told that in heaven we will be worshipping God himself.[37] There will be people there from every nation, tribe, people and language in the whole world, praising God together.[38] There will be 'no more death or mourning or crying or pain'.[39]

So heaven in the New Testament is not seen primarily as a reward for something, but rather as being with God. People will be given new resurrection bodies like the resurrection body of Jesus. So they will know and experience God in a deeper way than they could ever do on earth. They will not be disembodied souls — a Greek idea! The whole of creation will be renewed — there will be, we are told, 'a new heaven and a new earth'.

Once we understand the solemn crossroads that we reach when we die or when Jesus comes again — whichever happens first — we can then understand why the whole teaching of Jesus concerning his second coming focused on two crucial points. First, Jesus said he was coming at an unexpected time. Second, we must always be ready for his coming. Are there any signs which might let us know that the coming of Jesus is very soon?

It is a curious fact that many people believe the second coming of Jesus will be immediately preceded by terrible wars and famines. Yet Jesus himself never said this. What he *did* say was that his followers would have to go through all kinds of testing and trials before his second coming. These would certainly include wars, famines, earthquakes, persecution and the appearance of false prophets, but Jesus said that 'such things must happen, but the end is still to come . . . all these are the beginning of birth pains'.[40]

In fact Jesus said that he would come when people did *not* expect him. He would come as unexpectedly as a thief in the night. 'Understand this: If the owner of the house had known at what time of night the thief was coming, he would have kept watch and would not have let his house be broken into. So you also must be ready, because the Son of Man will come at an hour you do *not* expect him.'[41]

His coming would be as unexpected as the flood which came in the time of Noah. People were eating and drinking and carrying on their normal, daily lives right up to the day that Noah entered the ark. It would be like that, said Jesus, at the time when he returned.[42]

So any speculation about the date is futile. Jesus said that no one on earth knows the date. Only God knows.[43] If you read any newspaper reports or hear of anyone claiming to know the exact date of the second coming of Jesus, you can be quite sure that these reports are untrue. The sensational books claiming to show certain events as 'signs' of when Jesus will come are a waste of time.

In fact Jesus only gave one very general sign that pointed to his imminent return. He said, 'This gospel of the kingdom will be preached in the whole world as a testimony to all nations, and then the end will come.'[44]

When the good news about God's reign taking place through the death and resurrection of Jesus has been proclaimed to all nations, Jesus will come again. Certainly that day is drawing rapidly nearer. We must be ready.

It has also been suggested that the foundation of the modern state of Israel in 1947 is a fulfilment of prophecy or a sign that Jesus is soon coming again. In fact, as we have already seen, Jesus taught precisely the opposite. Whenever someone tried to

claim that Jesus had come to save specifically the nation of Israel,
Jesus made it quite clear that the good news about the kingdom
of God was equally for all nations. No one has any kind of special
privileges in the sight of God.

For example, when those two disciples on the road to Emmaus
had told the risen Jesus that they had thought that he was the one
who was going to save *Israel*, Jesus told them bluntly that they
were foolish![45] He said they were very slow to believe what the
prophets had said. Unfortunately there are plenty of people who
have been equally slow and foolish since that time.

Just before Jesus ascended into heaven, his disciples were still
asking him when he was going to 'restore the kingdom to Israel'
— in other words overthrow the power of Rome over the Jews.[46]
But Jesus told them not to speculate about dates that were known
by God alone. Instead they should immediately become involved
in the real meaning of God's kingdom, which was to spread the
message of the kingdom 'to the ends of the earth'. God's reign is
equally for all nations.

What we can be quite sure about is that the radical teaching of
Jesus on love and justice is applicable in every place and at every
time. People who forcibly take homes and land from others will
have to face the punishment of God when Jesus comes again.
Those who oppress the poor or who neglect the rights of minorities or who commit massacres will one day shake at the feet of
almighty God.

God is a consuming fire. Jesus is coming soon. Time is running
out. Only fools are not ready.

1   Acts 1:1–9
2   Luke 24:45–49
3   Luke 24:49; Acts 1:5
4   John 16:7–11
5   John 14:15–21
6   John 14:18–19
7   John 14:26; John 16:13
8   John 15:26
9   John 16:7–11
10 Acts 1:10–11
11 Luke 24:53

12   Acts 1:15–26
13   Acts 2:1–4
14   Matthew 3:11
15   Acts 2:14–21
16   Acts 2:22–37
17   Acts 2:38–39
18   Acts 2:41
19   Acts 3:1–10
20   For example see Acts 4:3–22; 5:17–42
21   Galatians 5:22–23
22   Acts 2:42–47
23   Acts 5:41
24   Acts 16:22–25
25   Acts 7:54–60
26   Acts 8
27   Acts 11:19–26
28   Matthew 24:27
29   Matthew 24:23–27
30   Matthew 24:30
31   Matthew 24:31
32   John 5:28–29
33   Matthew 7:1–2
34   Matthew 5:21–22, 27–30
35   Matthew 25:46
36   John 17:3
37   Revelation 4:1–11
38   Revelation 7:9–12
39   Revelation 21:4
40   Matthew 24:6, 8
41   Matthew 24:43–44
42   Matthew 24:37–41
43   Matthew 24:36
44   Matthew 24:14
45   Luke 24:21, 25
46   Acts 1:6–8

11

How to Enter the Kingdom of God

As we have seen, the central meaning of 'the kingdom of God' is the 'reign of God'. How do we submit to God's rule or reign over us? There is certainly no formula or programme that automatically transfers us into God's kingdom. But there are some key points which may help, and I will now try to explain these under four main headings, or steps. Lastly we will consider the results of entering the kingdom.

We are not talking here about anyone 'changing their religion'. Jesus did not come to change anyone's religion. Nor are we talking about changing our culture, or our name, or our loyalty to our country or community. We are considering something far bigger and far more important — our relationship with the God of the whole universe himself.

Step 1 Recognizing certain facts

Fact 1   God is absolutely holy and entering his kingdom means that we are willing to accept the standards of his holiness for our lives. As we have seen, God's holiness refers not just to the fact that he is far from us and completely different from us, but in particular to the fact that in his presence there can be no sin. That is a central characteristic of his being. It is something that has been proclaimed by all true prophets of God all down the centuries.

When Moses (Musa) went up on the mountain to receive the Ten Commandments, the sign that he was given of the presence of God was a consuming fire.[1] When God's Spirit came on the disciples at Pentecost, the sign given was again a fire.[2] God's holiness is a burning fire, and anything unholy brought into this presence will be immediately consumed.

Heaven is where God is. So a person can only go to heaven if they are made holy like God. Heaven for a person not made holy would be like hell, because that unholy person could not stand for one second in God's presence without being burned up. Remember what happened in the story of Jesus to the guest at the wedding feast who was not wearing the garment he had been given.[3]

Fact 2   We are sinners who have fallen far below the standards of God's holiness. We have gone over this central point in the teachings of Jesus on several occasions, especially in chapter six, and you may wish to review those pages if this teaching is not yet clear.

. Sin is not just a question of doing certain particularly bad things, such as murder, adultery, and so on, but instead refers to that whole process by which we place our own wills at the centre of our lives in the place of God's will. Sin refers to all those countless ways in which we have not really submitted to God. Throughout this book we have pictured it as a spiritual cancer eating away at the human heart.

You may or may not feel guilty when you realize that you have fallen so far short of God's standards of holiness. Some people can do terrible things and not feel guilty at all. Others can make some minor mistake and be overcome with guilt feelings. But what is important is not the feeling of guilt but the fact of sin.

As you understand the holiness of God you must accept the fact of moral guilt before God. Whether you feel guilty or not is really beside the point.

Imagine that you are in a court of law. The judge has listed all those ways in which you are selfish, unloving, impatient, irritable, deceitful, lustful, insensitive and greedy — in other words, all the ways in which you have fallen short of God's holiness. All you can plead is 'guilty'. There is no other logical plea to make under the circumstances, because we really are responsible for our lives.

It is surprising how difficult many people find it to plead 'guilty' before God. They still think that they are really quite nice people. Because their concept of God's holiness is not much larger than a peanut, they remain under the false impression that all is well and that a few minor reforms will correct any imperfections that remain.

We have looked at the teaching of Jesus on this issue in more detail in chapter six. But unless you are willing to plead 'guilty' before a holy God, read no further, because you are wasting your time.

Fact 3   We cannot go to heaven by means of our good deeds. If you are willing to accept the first two facts about the holiness of God and human sin, then this follows logically as the dawn follows the night.

If heaven means God's presence, then clearly it is absurd to expect that our good deeds will be sufficient to take us there. We have also covered the teaching of Jesus on this matter at some length in chapter six.

If you are trying to leap from one side of a ravine to another, it does not make much difference whether you fall short by twenty meters, five meters or one meter. The result is the same. You fall into the ravine. Different people may fall short of God's holiness to different degrees, but the point is that they have all fallen short.

Sometimes people ask me what I think about a particular great prophet or famous religious teacher. My reply is nearly always the same: 'Their teaching is fine as far as it goes.' There is a tremendous amount of good moral and ethical teaching that we can obtain from nearly all the great religious leaders of the world. But none of this teaching solves the basic problem of man's sin. Doing more and more good deeds does not solve the cancer of sin.

It is like someone with a physical cancer being told that they should take pain-killing drugs, continue to dress nicely, carry on working as long as possible, and still be kind to people. There is nothing wrong with any of these things, but the advice is not very relevant to curing the cancer.

Once you understand that you are suffering from the fatal spiritual cancer of sin, then you will not be content with any superficial answers to your problem. You will realize that all your good deeds and religious observances are like the shadows made by the full moon, which look so impressive in the night, but which quickly fade to nothing once the sun rises.

Fact 4   Jesus is God's way of salvation. For many this will be the hardest fact of all to accept, because they may have been brought up with the idea that Jesus was just a prophet or a religious teacher. It is certainly true that when we have been taught certain things since we were children, then it is harder to change those beliefs in later life.

That is why it is helpful if you can take the attitude of a scientist in looking at the life and teachings of Jesus of Nazareth. This involves a willingness to look at his claims with an open mind, ready to be persuaded one way or the other. I am sure that we can all think of other 'facts' we heard when we were children, and which perhaps we continued to believe for a very long time, yet which, in later life, we found were untrue. I do hope that you are tolerant and open-minded enough to at least consider that this *may* be the case when it comes to all the negative stories about the claims of Jesus you may have heard as a child — or the television gurus who dismiss his claims as myths and legends.

I am sure you will have to agree with me that *if* the claims of Jesus are indeed true, then either his coming to earth is the greatest event in history, or else the whole story of his life and teachings that we have been explaining in this book so far is complete rubbish. If the one almighty God has appeared among human beings in the form of a man, then by definition this one great act must be the central point of our attention. It would be absurd to think otherwise. But if it is not true, do not think that we can learn anything from the morality or ethics of Jesus, because clearly he was then the greatest liar that ever lived, having totally deceived a very large proportion of the world's population during the past 2,000 years.

What does it mean to accept that Jesus is God's way of salvation? It means that we have to accept Jesus for who he is, and we have to accept what he has done for us through his death and resurrection.

Who is Jesus? I can only refer you back to chapter seven in which we considered his claims. The really important point is to see the spiritual continuity between Jesus and God. Unless that continuity is true, Jesus is no king: his kingdom is nothing but false promises. Unless it is true, then we are travelling down a dead-end street, because one person cannot take away the sins of another. Only God can take away sin. If God was not in Jesus in that great sacrifice of the cross, then it was just a meaningless death, with no ultimate significance for us in the twentieth century.

I am not asking you to *understand* the exact relationship between Jesus and God. Many people do not realize how little scientists understand of various phenomena which we have to accept in our daily lives. For example, when I press the light switch, the light goes on, but our understanding of how electricity flows along the wire is still very rudimentary. Even such a common force as gravity remains largely a mystery. We all look forward to the day when one 'grand theory' will unite all the fundamental forces of the universe, but that day has not arrived yet. If this is the situation with the physical forces that we utilize every day of our lives, how much more should we expect true mysteries in our concept of God?

The early followers of Jesus had a simple creed or statement which expressed their faith in Jesus. It comes out in just three words in English: 'Jesus is Lord.'

So when Peter first preached the good news of the kingdom to some Roman soldiers in Palestine, we read that he was 'Telling the good news of peace through Jesus Christ (the Messiah) who is *Lord of all.*'[4]

Proclaiming 'Jesus is Lord' was a revolutionary statement for a monotheistic Jew. It meant a whole change in world-view, a turning upside down of all his previously-held beliefs. During the first few centuries after Jesus, saying this in public in the wrong place at the wrong time was quite sufficient for a person to be crucified or thrown to hungry lions. At that time the emperor in Rome was seen as the only 'Lord', so the creed 'Jesus is Lord' was seen as a direct challenge to the authority of Rome.

Accepting that Jesus is King or Lord is an essential step in order to enter the kingdom of God. Unless we accept who Jesus is, his death and resurrection will have no meaning for us, because if his claims are false there is still no bridge to God. Of course, if we accept the historical evidence for his resurrection, that is the ultimate seal and confirmation of the truth of his claims. So we can see that the life, death, and resurrection of Jesus all come together as one unified whole, and every aspect of the whole is vital for the fulfilment of God's great plan of salvation in our lives.

To enter the kingdom of God means accepting the historical fact of the sacrifice of Jesus on the cross to take away sin. That means that Jesus died for our sin. He demonstrated the love of God by this total involvement and identification with human suffering.

By rising from the dead Jesus showed that he had conquered death and defeated the power of evil once and for all. The resurrection of Jesus from the dead was a historical event which was the demonstration of the power of God to overcome all satanic, demonic and human opposition to his reign and authority.

The way of the death and resurrection of Jesus of Nazareth is the very door into heaven. That is why Jesus said, 'I am the way, the truth, and the life. No one comes to the Father except through me.'[5]

So by his death Jesus has won our freedom from the guilt and penalty of sin. By his resurrection he has made possible a new quality of life, the 'eternal life' of the kingdom. It vindicates his teaching about the kingdom: a whole new start for a fallen world, a new beginning — starting with himself. It is a process that one day will be completed when Jesus returns and all things will be made new. Do we want to be part of this amazing way of salvation?

God, because of his great love, is offering us this great salvation. It is a free gift. Love always gives, it never forces. God will never force salvation on anyone. Jesus' sacrifice on the cross does not bring automatic forgiveness for everyone. The *potential* for forgiveness is there, but it only becomes real in the life of the individual as he accepts the gift for himself.

Even if you have agreed with all the facts that we have talked about so far — the holiness of God, human sin, the impossibility of going to heaven by good deeds, the final solution to sin brought about by God through the death and resurrection of Jesus the Son of Man, the new kingdom of God — accepting these facts by themselves does not take you into the kingdom. Instead, agreeing with the facts is like having a launching pad ready and in position before the rocket actually takes off . . .

Step 2 Counting the Cost

Jesus talked a lot about the cost of accepting God's reign. When large crowds of people were following him, he said to them, 'Anyone who does not carry his cross and follow me cannot be my disciple.'[6]

Following Jesus means travelling the way he travelled. Of course for most people that does not mean literal crucifixion, but it does mean death to the old life of sin and resurrection into the new life of the kingdom. 'Taking up the cross' does not refer to some special problem or difficulty that we may have, but to the whole process whereby God's will is placed in the centre of our lives. That means a 'crossing out' of our old selfish ways. In English it so happens that the shape of the cross is an 'I' crossed out. That summarizes what 'taking up the cross' means very neatly.

On the same occasion that Jesus talked about people carrying their cross and following him, he went on to say, 'Suppose one of you wants to build a tower. Will he not first sit down and estimate the cost to see if he has enough money to complete it? For if he lays the foundation and is not able to finish it, everyone who sees it will ridicule him saying, 'This fellow began to build and was not able to finish.'[7]

It is not difficult to think of half-finished buildings, lying derelict with weeds growing inside. They have no roofs, windows or doors, so are useless as homes. Someone began to build without counting the cost.

Jesus said that we must understand the cost of the kingdom *before* we enter.

You may remember that we have already begun in chapter five to look at the story of the rich young ruler.[8] The ruler asked

Jesus, 'Good Teacher, what must I do to inherit eternal life?'

The ruler clearly thought that Jesus was just another religious teacher and probably wanted to add the teaching of Jesus to the collection of wise sayings from various religious leaders that he had no doubt memorized.

The reply of Jesus was surprising: 'Why do you call me good? No one is good — except God alone.'

Then you will remember that Jesus went on to list several of the Ten Commandments which related to social relationships.

'All these I have kept since I was a boy', said the ruler.

We might well say the same. We have not committed adultery or murdered anybody. We have never stolen anything and always try to respect our parents . . .

But then Jesus continued, 'You still lack one thing. Sell everything you have and give it to the poor, and you will have treasure in heaven. Then come, follow me.'

When the rich young ruler heard this, he became very sad, because he was wealthy. Jesus looked at him and said, 'How hard it is for the rich to enter the kingdom of God! Indeed, it is easier for a camel to go through the eye of a needle than for a rich man to enter the kingdom of God!'

Jesus was not telling the ruler that if he gave up his riches, then he would receive eternal life in exchange. In the first commandment, God says, 'You shall have no other gods before me.'[9]

The ruler did in fact have another 'god'. His riches took central place in his life. Whatever takes central place in our life is our god. We may say nice phrases with our lips, but if our hearts are gripped by the love of something apart from God then we are breaking the first commandment.

So no one should be deceived into thinking that they can enter God's kingdom and then live just as they did before. It will mean Jesus and his kingdom power released by God's Holy Spirit into that person's life having absolute first place. This is no easy option.

It may help us to understand the extent of that cost when we remember that, according to Jesus, there are only two 'kingdoms' in the whole world. First there is Satan's kingdom, the power of evil. We are all born into Satan's kingdom because we are all born under the power of sin. As we saw in chapter six, we do not become sinful by sinning after a certain critical age. Rather we are born with a tendency to sin, and we continue to be dominated by that tendency until a greater power rescues us from it.

That greater power is the might of God himself who, through the death and resurrection of Jesus, enables us to be transferred into his kingdom. So as we pass from Satan's kingdom of darkness into God's kingdom of light, we are taking a giant step which is for all eternity. There is no going back.

Step 3 Repentance

We have already discussed what John the Baptist and Jesus himself had to say about repentance in chapters two and three. You will remember that repentance involves changing direction. A soldier is marching in one direction. The sergeant shouts out 'About turn' and the soldier goes in the opposite direction. That is repentance.

Repentance also involves true sorrow for the sin in our lives. It may be accompanied by a feeling of guilt, but a feeling of guilt is not necessary in order to repent. However, as we saw before, accepting the *fact* of our guilt is vital. As we repent, we come to God and confess how far short we have fallen from his commands. We ask his forgiveness. We decide to turn in a new direction in our lives — the direction of submission to God and the way that Jesus taught.

Sometimes repentance may be a very emotional experience. I have seen tough men on their knees repenting in tears as they realized how far they were from the living God, and how deeply they were trapped in their own selfishness and sin. For other people repentance is not at all emotional, but more like a logical acceptance of the facts of the situation in which they recognize their moral guilt before God and express sorrow for their disobedience.

Whether it is emotional or not is really not important, but what *is* important is our depth of commitment as we repent. Do we mean it? Is it just nice words, or does it come from our innermost beings? Only time will tell.

Be very sure that there is no hope of entering the kingdom of God without repentance. From the very beginning of his public ministry, Jesus proclaimed to the people, 'The time has come. The kingdom of God is near. *Repent* and believe the good news!'[10]

When Jesus sent out the twelve disciples into the towns and villages of Palestine, 'they went out and preached that people should *repent*.'[11]

When Jesus was talking about the Galileans who had met a terrible death, he warned the crowds, 'But unless you *repent*, you too will all perish.'[12]

Repentance was still one of the central themes of the disciples as they preached to the crowds after Pentecost: '*Repent*, then, and turn to God, so that your sins may be wiped out.'[13]

The spirit of true repentance is captured well in this story which Jesus told:

'Two men went up to the temple to pray, one a Pharisee and the other a tax collector. The Pharisee stood up and prayed about himself: "God, I thank you that I am not like all other men — robbers, evildoers, adulterers — or even like this tax collector. I fast twice a week and give a tenth of all I get."

'But the tax collector stood at a distance. He would not even look up to heaven, but beat his breast and said, "God, have mercy on me, a sinner." '[14]

Jesus went on to say that it was the despised tax collector that was accepted in the sight of God, not the proud Pharisee.

Repentance means not only accepting our guilt, but also doing something about it. It involves that most difficult step of all — losing face. In that one little word 'sorry' is more explosive force than in a thousand bombs . . .

Step 4 Faith

Let us imagine that you have accepted these basic facts about our situation that we mentioned in step one. Let us say that you have counted the cost, and have lifted up your arms to almighty God as you repented and confessed your guilt and sin to him. There is one remaining crucial act of commitment which will now take you right into God's kingdom. That is 'faith'.

Faith means so many different things to so many different people, that it will take a little while to explain what Jesus meant by the word.

One clue comes from the occasion when the disciples of Jesus were asking him who would be greatest in the kingdom of heaven.[15] Jesus replied by calling a little child to stand in the centre of the group. Then he said, 'Unless you change and become like little children, you will never enter the kingdom of heaven. Therefore, whoever humbles himself like this little child is the greatest in the kingdom of heaven.'

Jesus was not saying that we had to share the ignorance or educational level of a child. But he was saying that we need the humble trust of the child.

A few months ago there was intensive shelling all round our house during the night. Our little girl looked up at her mother as they sheltered together in the corridor and said, 'I'm happy mummy.' As long as her parents were there, everything was all right, whatever noises might be coming from outside.

You see the same attitude of humble trust when small children have to cross a busy road. They put their hand in the hand of one of their parents and cheerfully cross through the dangerous traffic.

That is what the New Testament means by 'faith' — a humble trust in God and in what he has done for us. Such faith involves commitment.

A surgeon had a patient who needed a serious operation. The patient told everybody that he was fully convinced that this particular surgeon was just the right man to carry out his operation. But when the day came, the patient refused to be given the anaesthetic. 'Why', he said, 'how do I know what will happen after I'm unconscious? What will the surgeon do to me then?'

The patient certainly had no real faith in the surgeon. He had plenty of nice words, but his lack of trust showed itself by his actions. Real faith always results in action.

Faith in Jesus is much more than agreeing to a certain set of beliefs. You can agree in your head with all the points that we summarized in step one, but without having faith. Faith means trust, commitment, obedience, that act of the will whereby you stake your whole life on the word of another.

On one occasion a man placed a tightrope right across the Niagara Falls in Canada. Then he jumped on the rope and walked across to the other side in front of a large crowd. After that he took a wheelbarrow and wheeled it across the roaring water. Everyone was amazed. When he had returned safely, he asked the crowd, 'How many of you believe that I could take a person across the falls safely inside my wheelbarrow?'

Everyone had seen how good he was. They had now seen him walk safely across the rope several times. So quite a few hands went up in the crowd.

'Very good', said the man . . . 'Could someone who raised their hand please jump in the wheelbarrow? I would like to take you across!'

For some reason there were no volunteers!

It is one thing to *believe* something, but it is quite another to have the kind of belief which results in action.

Entering the kingdom of God is quite impossible without such humble trust. But it is not faith itself which saves us. It is the object of our faith which is the key. It is God who saves by means of our faith. Faith is that agreement, commitment and humble trust whereby we accept his plan of salvation through Jesus for our lives. We are like the small child who throws himself into his father's arms, knowing that he will receive love and acceptance.

Faith certainly becomes much easier when we know that we have a heavenly Father who loves us with a love which is far beyond human understanding. God never rejects the person who comes to him in faith.

Faith means trusting that the sacrifice of Jesus on the cross was fully sufficient to take away your sin. It means relying on him for forgiveness as you come to God in repentance. It involves thanking God for such a wonderful salvation and then asking Jesus himself to be the new Lord of your life. If your life is like a house, then it is like handing over all the keys of your life to Jesus. No rooms can remain locked when he is invited in to bring his light and love. You hand every department of your life over to him.

Faith is certainly not a blind leap into the dark. In many ways it is the exact opposite. What could be more logical and sensible than putting our lives totally in the hands of the creator of the whole universe? The same God who creates his universe in such an ordered and systematic way is the one who also makes a perfect plan of salvation for our lives.

Faith is not trying to believe in something even though there is little evidence for it, but rather the response of our wills to the overwhelming evidence which faces us. Both the facts and the meaning of the death and resurrection of Jesus are so well-established that faith based on these great acts of God in history can never be 'blind'. Where childlike trust is essential is in believing that God is going to take us right into his kingdom on the basis of those facts. It is that faith which believes that Jesus is going to come right into the centre of our lives as we invite him in to be our own Lord and Saviour, even though we cannot physically see him.

As Jesus said to doubting Thomas, 'Blessed are those who have not seen and yet have believed.'[16]

It is not by the amount of our faith that we enter the kingdom, as if faith is like some fluid which could be quantified. Neither is faith some *feeling* of trust which we have to work up inside us. Nor is faith something that we can receive from our parents, friends or environment. It is not inherited, as if some lucky people 'have faith' and others do not.

No, faith is that act of the will whereby we trust what God has said and done, and then act on the basis of his promises. As Jesus said at the last supper with his disciples, 'This is my blood of the "covenant" which is poured out for many for the forgiveness of sins.'[17]

Faith is believing that God's promises in this new 'agreement' or 'covenant' really are true. There is real forgiveness of sins.

I can give you no special formula for repenting of your sin and putting your faith or trust in the living Jesus. You can pray to God in your own words at any place and at any time. You can be alone or with others. It really makes no difference. Neither does it matter if your prayer is very simple. The important point is whether you really mean it. God knows us through and through. Nothing is hidden from him. We can fool others. We can even fool ourselves. But we cannot fool God.

At the moment we really repent and put our trust in Jesus to save and forgive us, then we enter the kingdom of God. This is a spiritual transaction between you and God. It is invisible to others. Indeed, you may feel exactly the same afterwards as you did before. Do not expect lightning from heaven! Your feelings are not as important as the promises of God.

When you enter the kingdom of God, certain crucial changes take place.

God forgives all your sins. On the basis of the sacrifice of Jesus on the cross alone, you are pardoned from every sin that you ever committed — with no exceptions. It is like starting life all over again with a clean slate. David spoke about God's forgiveness in this way: 'As far as the east is from the west, so far has he removed our sins from us.'[18] That is what God does as you enter his kingdom — he totally removes all your sins.

Does that mean that you will now live a sinless life for the rest of your days? Unfortunately not! However much we continue to struggle against sin, there will be times when we fall. But when you do sin, there is now a basis for forgiveness. You can keep going back to God and each time base your plea for mercy and forgiveness upon what Jesus did for you through his death and resurrection.

As one of the disciples of Jesus wrote: 'If we claim to be without sin, we deceive ourselves and the truth is not in us. If we confess our sins, he is faithful and just and will forgive us our sins.'[19]

The important point is to keep confessing our sin and not try to hide it either from ourselves or from God (he knows all about it anyway).

Sometimes a very short while after someone has entered the kingdom of God they face the most incredible temptations. Just as Jesus had to face his greatest temptations just after starting his public ministry, so often Satan launches a vicious counter-offensive against us as soon as we leave his kingdom of darkness. Do not be surprised when these attacks come.

If you do fall at any time, do not forget to return immediately to God afresh in repentance and faith. He will immediately cleanse you again because of the cross, and then you just keep fighting that spiritual battle which is now a part of your daily life.

God's kingdom is, in fact, a kingdom of forgiveness. You are forgiven as you enter, and you are forgiven as you continue on in your new relationship with God.

God justifies you. 'Justify' is a legal word which means to 'declare right' or 'to declare righteous'. When a prisoner has completed his prison sentence and is set free, he is 'justified' because he has gone through the punishment that the judge decided to give him. When a person enters God's kingdom, he is 'justified' before God because the penalty for his sin has been paid by Jesus. So God 'declares him righteous' on the basis of the death and resurrection of Jesus.

It is like the people who were given wedding garments in the 'wedding feast' story of Jesus mentioned in chapter eight. The guests did not deserve to be invited to the feast. They were not those originally invited anyway. But they were all there on the same basis by the 'grace' of the king. By giving them all the same special garments, the king declared them both invited and welcomed as his own special guests. When we are justified by God as we enter his kingdom, it is like receiving a white 'garment of salvation' which covers all our filthy rags. As the King looks at us, he sees not our old lives of selfishness and sin, but our new garment which has been given to us by Jesus himself. We are justified in his sight.

Being 'justified' by God happens only once — at the time that we enter his kingdom. It is actually the starting-point of our new relationship with him. It is the foundation-stone for our growth in the new life of God's Spirit. It is the irreversible 'legal process' whereby we are made a child of God.

God makes you his child. Coming into God's kingdom is like becoming part of God's family. By coming to know God as our heavenly Father, we experience the reality of being like one of his own children.

The New Testament calls this 'adoption'. Before we come to know God, we are like spiritual orphans. But through repentance and faith God 'adopts' us into the spiritual family of his kingdom. We become part of a new world-wide community of those who have experienced his forgiveness through Jesus.

When Jesus was explaining God's true path of salvation to Nicodemus, the member of the Jewish council, Jesus told him that entering God's kingdom was like being born all over again.[20] The new birth results in a new family. All those who have passed through the same door of forgiveness are your brothers and sisters.

Being a child of God means you have access to your heavenly Father in prayer. Prayer is talking to God. A loving human father will always have time to spend listening to his children. How much more is our heavenly Father willing not only to listen but also to answer our prayers!

Being a child of God also means we can lose the fear and worry from our lives. There are plenty of things that can make us afraid in the world in which we live — fear of sickness or death, fear of not getting married, fear of what other people think about us, fear of failure, fear about our studies, our job . . . When Jesus comes into our lives, he comes to remove the whole basis for fear. God is now our loving heavenly Father who cares for us as his own personal children. He knows exactly what the future holds for us. So we can leave the future in his hands. That is not fatalism: it is an act of trust in the goodness of God.

Once you know that you are a child of God, you then possess another very good reason for being sure that salvation really is yours for all eternity. Your adoption into God's family is *his* work. And what God brings to pass cannot be undone. You cannot be un-adopted once you have been welcomed by God into his family. We may act like a naughty child, or a rebellious child, or neglect our family — but we still stay a member of the family!

God gives you his Holy Spirit. The moment of repentance and faith is the same moment that God's Holy Spirit enters your life. You are 'immersed' in God's Spirit in the same way that the disciples were on the day of Pentecost. The Spirit may not come with the same drama, but he certainly comes with the same power. You may or may not *feel* different after his coming upon you, but you may be very sure of his presence with you from now on.

Remember that life in the kingdom is a life of faith — of steady trust in God's promises — whether we have immediate visible signs of his presence or not.

The most important evidence of the Holy Spirit's work in your life will take some time to appear. That is the fruit of the Spirit. Fruit does not appear on trees as soon as spring arrives. There has to be the blossom and the spring rains, followed by a maturing process as the green fruit becomes ripe. So with the fruit of the Spirit. It will take time, but as you live day by day in your new and close relationship to God, so the fruit will surely come.

One of the central tasks of the Holy Spirit in your life is to make you holy. The Spirit begins to make you in practice what God has already declared you to be by faith.

There was once a king who had no heir to his throne. As he was becoming old, he had almost despaired of having children. An orphan boy used to come begging at the kitchen door of the palace. One day the king happened to see this boy out in the backyard. The boy was dressed in rags and his hands were blue with cold. 'Why', said the king to himself, 'here is a poor boy with no parents of his own. I could adopt him as my own son and train him myself to become the heir to my throne.'

And that is exactly what the king did. He invited the poor boy in personally and proceeded to dress him in his finest clothes. He put a crown on his head and proclaimed him to all the people as his very own adopted son.

Of course it is one thing to make such a declaration, but it is quite another for the adopted one to start actually behaving like the king's son! At the beginning, the orphan behaved just as he did before — he ate with his mouth open, had no table manners, could not keep himself clean, and had the most terrible language! None of this behaviour altered the *fact* of his adoption as the king's son, but it took a long time before the king's own effective training helped him to behave as a king's son should behave.

So it is with a person who is adopted as God's own child. 'Justification' is the declaration of the fact that God's law has no accusation to make against him because of the death and resurrection of Jesus. The person is *declared* to be righteous because of what God has done for him. God's Spirit then comes into that person's life to *make* him righteous. The person is adopted into God's family. Nothing can change his legal status. But the process of learning to live in a holy way is one that will last the rest of his life.

So the Holy Spirit produces God's fruit, guides us in our lives, gives us power to resist Satan's temptations, makes our consciences come alive so that we know when we have sinned, and gives to us gifts that we can use in service for others. The Holy Spirit is God in action, working out his plan for our lives.

God promises you eternal life. In one sense, when you believe in Jesus as the Messiah, it is as if you are symbolically going through the history that he went through.

When we put our faith in Jesus, our old life died with him on the cross. The 'old person' that we were before that moment of repentance and faith is crucified with Jesus. As Jesus rose from the dead, so we too rise to newness of life, eternal life, when we enter the kingdom of God. After that we experience the resurrection power of Jesus in our lives through his Spirit. Jesus reproduces in us by his Holy Spirit the very same works of love and power which he himself performed when he was on earth.

But the story does not end there. Those who have entered God's kingdom will also share in the resurrection of the body, the new creation worked out in time, when Jesus comes again. No longer is there any need to fear death. Jesus said, 'I tell you the truth, whoever hears my word and believes him who sent me has eternal life and will not be condemned; he has crossed over from death to life.'[21]

The risen Jesus lives in each person who is a part of God's family. This is the guarantee that the person will be given an eternal resurrection body like that of Jesus himself when he finally comes again. And if the person dies before that great event, then he will go straight to heaven. There is no question of any further 'perfecting' needing to be done. The resurrected Jesus is living in him. That is the basis for his going to heaven, not anything that he may have done himself.

The moment of repentance and faith is just the first page of the 'story of salvation' that God begins to write about our new life in his kingdom. And just as God writes the first page, so he also will write the last page. Salvation is his work. Our task is the path of submission to what he has done, is doing and will do in the future in our lives. You cannot separate the present from the past, nor the present from the future in God's kingdom. God has saved, is saving us, and will save us — these are the three tenses of salvation. As surely as there has been death to the old person that we were before, so surely there will be physical resurrection to life in heaven with God for all eternity.

To explain all the results of entering God's kingdom would take another book! Here I shall underline just two key points:

From now on we enjoy fellowship with God. When God originally created us, it was for fellowship with himself. This purpose was thwarted when 'in Adam' we chose to go our own way rather than God's way. Now, 'in Christ', the barrier to fellowship with God has been removed. We can worship him for all that he is. We can 'enjoy him for ever'. We can enter into the true reason for our existence.

What is worship? Worship is giving that honour, praise, respect and adoration which is due to the Creator of the whole universe. It is far more than going through certain prayers or obeying various religious laws. It is the whole process whereby we bring glory to God by being in submission to his will.

Jesus said that the Father was looking for those who would worship God 'in spirit and in truth'.[22] That is the great motivation for living a life of holiness once we have entered God's kingdom. We want to be holy in order to bring glory to the holy God.

Despite all that we have said so far, you may still feel that receiving salvation as a free gift is a very dangerous possibility. Surely, you may say, if someone has already received salvation which also guarantees them a future resurrection to eternal life, then they can go out and sin as much as they want? But if a person thinks in that way, this shows how little they have understood of the kingdom of God! God's reign demands everything we have. Death and burial of our lives with Jesus and resurrection to new life in the Spirit means death to sin! True worship means offering up our lives as a daily sacrifice to God.

Love is the key. As we come to know God, so we are entering a new relationship based on love. God loves us so much, even

though we do not deserve it, and we respond to his love in glad
surrender to his will. As coming to know God is begun in love, so
that deepening knowledge of him continues in love. We do not
wish to please him because he is like a cruel tyrant with a stick
who will beat us for our smallest mistake. We want to worship
God because we love him.

After I was married, I did not put up a long list of rules and
regulations for my wife, saying 'you will make the beds, you will
go out to work, you must keep the house clean, and so on'. The
marriage relationship should be based on love, not on law. We
try to please each other because we love one another.

We want to please and honour God because we love him. Of
course his laws are fixed and unchanging. The Ten Commandments are just as true as when they were first given. But the heavy
burden of trying to obey the law is no longer present. We discover
that they are God's ways for healthy, fulfilled living! We have
become captives to God's love and want to do what *he* wants.

**We become part of a worldwide community of those who share a
common life.** As we have seen, God's purposes have involved
calling a new people for himself. He has forgiven them, given
them new life, given them gifts by his Holy Spirit.

So he has created a new community, the church, which
expresses the life of the kingdom, the life of the future, here and
now. It is worldwide. It is also very practical: a local gathering of
those who join for fellowship and teaching, for worship and
prayer, for baptism and communion, for sharing the faith with
others.

At the beginning, such groups met in private homes to pray
together and remember the death and resurrection of Jesus in the
Lord's Supper, as Jesus had told them to do — see chapter eight.
Not surprisingly, with time, the word 'church' came to refer to
the building in which they met. But that was not its original
meaning.

Jesus in fact gave no rules as to how people should worship
God when they were together in groups. He left no instructions
about the method of praying, apart from giving a sample prayer
that we have quoted in chapter four. He laid down no rules about
how much money you should keep for yourself and how much

you should give to others in need.

This means that people who share a common life in God's kingdom are free to express their worship together in a way relevant to their own culture. We may like to bang on drums and make a big noise to express our joy as we worship God with others. Or we may want to worship God in silent prayer and with periods of meditation. One way of worship is not 'better' than the other. It is simply a question of expressing the true worship of our hearts.

Many people think that because they have seen believers in Jesus worshipping in a certain way in one country, then this must be the way for believers in all countries. This has led to the situation where people have imported a way of worship from somewhere else which may not fit very well with the local culture, or may even be offensive to some people. In such cases it is better to do without the 'imported variety' and make sure that one's own community worship is home-grown. There is enough economic and political imperialism without importing cultural imperialism into our churches as well!

The task of a community of believers is to demonstrate the life of God's kingdom together. One aspect of this community is communal worship — but there are many other aspects as well. The community will demonstrate God's concern for the poor and the oppressed, for the socially neglected and the sick. As an early follower of Jesus put it: 'If anyone has material possessions and sees his brother in need but has no pity on him, how can the love of God be in him?'[23]

The new community of the kingdom will demonstrate God's love in practice. Believers will seek to love not only their friends, but also their enemies as well.

So the community should be like a signpost to God's kingdom, demonstrating his reign on earth by living together in glad submission to that reign. One day all remaining opposition to the kingdom of God will be finally abolished when Jesus comes again. Until that great day comes, communities of believers in Jesus have a great responsibility to bring the future life of the kingdom right into the present evil age in which we are now living. The life that they demonstrate together should be like the perfume of those flowers mentioned in chapter three, drifting in through the open door from the garden beyond. . .

We began this book with a small baby entering the world in a typical home in first-century Palestine. That baby was destined to be God's chosen channel whereby his kingdom power would break into the world and become available for all those who put their trust in him. The ripples from that crucial event in history are still spreading outwards to touch countless millions of people with a new way of love which is stronger than hate.

Are we ourselves willing to be touched by that love?

1   Exodus 24:15–18
2   Acts 2:1–4
3   Matthew 22:1–14
4   Acts 10:36
5   John 14:6
6   Luke 14:27
7   Luke 14:28–30
8   Luke 18:18–27
9   Exodus 20:3
10 Mark 1:15
11 Mark 6:12
12 Luke 13:3
13 Acts 3:19
14 Luke 18:10–13
15 Matthew 18:1–5
16 John 20:29
17 Matthew 26:28
18 Psalm 103:12
19 1 John 1:8–9
20 John 3:1–21
21 John 5:24
22 John 4:23–24
23 1 John 3:17